DATE DUE

A GUIDE TO CRITICAL THINKING

SELECTED CHAPTERS FROM FIFTH AND NINTH EDITIONS

PHILOSOPHY 11

RIVERSIDE CITY COLLEGE

VINCENT RYAN RUGGIERO
PROFESSOR EMERITUS OF HUMANITIES
STATE UNIVERSITY OF NEW YORK, DELHI

Mc Graw Hill **Learning Solutions**

Boston   Burr Ridge, IL   Dubuque, IA   New York   San Francisco   St. Louis
Bangkok   Bogotá   Caracas   Lisbon   London   Madrid
Mexico City   Milan   New Delhi   Seoul   Singapore   Sydney   Taipei   Toronto

Beyond Feelings: A Guide to Critical Thinking
Philosophy 11
Riverside Community College

This book is a McGraw-Hill Learning Solutions textbook and contains select
material from the following sources:
Beyond Feelings: A Guide to Critical Thinking, Fifth Edition by Vincent Ryan
Ruggiero. Copyright © 1998 by The McGraw-Hill Companies, Inc.
Beyond Feelings: A Guide to Critical Thinking, Ninth Edition by Vincent Ryan
Ruggiero..Copyright © 2012 by The McGraw-Hill Companies, Inc.
Both reprinted with permission of the publisher. Many custom published texts are
modified versions or adaptations of our best-selling textbooks. Some adaptations are
printed in black and white to keep prices at a minimum, while others are in color.

8 9 0 BRP BRP 16

ISBN-13: 978-0-07-782004-6
ISBN-10: 0-07-782004-5

Learning Solutions Consultant: Kimberly Scheyving
Learning Solutions Representative: Jennifer Beecher
Project Manager: Heather Ervolino
Printer/Binder: BR Printers- California

To the memory of Howard Trumble,
whose quiet practice of the skills
detailed in this book was an inspiration
to me, to his family, and to all who knew him.

Contents

Preface

When the first edition of this book appeared in 1975, the dominant intellectual focus was still subjectivity, *feelings*. That focus, the legacy of the 1960s, was originally a necessary reaction to the rationalism and behaviorism that preceded it. It declared, in effect: "People are not robots. They are more than the sum total of their physiology. They have hopes, dreams, emotions. No two humans are alike—each has a special perspective, a unique way of perceiving the world. And any view of humanity that ignores this subjective side is a distortion."

Yet, despite its value, the focus on feelings went too far. Like many other movements, what began as a reaction against an extreme view became an extreme view itself. The result of that extremism was the neglect of thinking. This book was designed to answer that neglect. The introduction to the first edition explained its rationale as follows:

> The emphasis on subjectivity served to correct a dangerous oversimplification. But it is the kind of reaction that cannot be sustained for long without causing an even worse situation—the neglect of thinking. Worse for two reasons. First, because we live in an age of manipulation. Armies of hucksters and demagogues stand ready with the rich resources of psychology to play upon our emotions and subconscious needs to persuade us that superficial is profound, harmful is beneficial, evil is virtuous. And feelings are especially vulnerable to such manipulation.
>
> Secondly, because in virtually every important area of modern life— law, medicine, government, education, science, business, and community affairs—we are beset with serious problems and complex issues that demand careful gathering and weighing of facts and informed opinions, thoughtful consideration of various conclusions or actions, and judicious selection of the best conclusion or most appropriate action. . . .
>
> [Today's college student] has been conditioned not to undervalue subjectivity, but to overvalue it. And so he does not need to have his feelings indulged. Rather, he needs to be taught how to sort out his feelings, decide to what extent they have been shaped by external influences, and

evaluate them carefully when they conflict among themselves or with the feelings of others. In short, he needs to be taught to think critically.*

There is an unfortunate tendency among many to view feeling and thought as mutually exclusive, to force a choice between them. If we focus on one, then in their view we must reject the other. But this is mistaken. Feeling and thought are perfectly complementary. Feeling, being more spontaneous, is an excellent beginning to the development of conclusions. And thought, being more deliberate, provides a way to identify the best and most appropriate feeling. Both are natural.

Thinking, however, is less automatic than feeling. To do it well demands a systematic approach and guided practice.

The general attitude toward thinking has changed considerably since the mid-1970s. The view that critical thinking is an important skill to which education should give prominence is no longer a minority view. Hundreds of voices have joined the chorus calling for the addition of critical thinking objectives to existing courses and even the creation of special courses in thinking. There is little disagreement that the challenges of the new millennium demand minds that can move beyond feelings to clear, impartial, critical problem solving and decision making.

Features of This Edition

This edition of *Beyond Feelings* retains the basic organization of previous editions. The first section explains the psychological, philosophical, and social context in which critical thinking takes place and describes the habits and attitudes that enhance such thinking. The second section helps students recognize and overcome common errors in thinking. The third section provides a step-by-step strategy for dealing with issues.

Within the overall design, however, I have made a number of changes, most in response to the helpful suggestions of reviewers.

- In Chapter 1, a new section—"The Influence of Ideas"—has been added.
- In Chapter 3, a new section—"Understanding Cause and Effect"— has been added.
- In Chapter 15, new examples of the value of observation have been added.
- In Chapter 17, the subsection "Evaluate your information sources" has been expanded.
- A number of new "Difference of Opinion" exercises have been added.

*In 1975, "he" was still accepted as a reference to both sexes.

As in the past, I have attempted to follow George Orwell's sage advice: "Never use a foreign phrase, a scientific word, or a jargon word if you can think of an everyday English equivalent." This is not always easy. When logicians are taught terms such as *argumentum ad hominem*, *non sequitur*, and "affirming the consequent," they naturally want to use them. Arguments for doing so urge themselves upon us: for example, "These are the most precise terms. Don't join the ranks of the coddlers and deprive students of them." In weak moments I succumb to this appeal. (Until the previous edition, for example, I included the term *enthymeme. Mea culpa . . .* there I go again.) But is the precision of such terms the real reason for my wanting to use them? Is it not possible that we professors enjoy parading our knowledge or that we are reluctant to spare our students the struggle we were forced to undergo ("We suffered, so they should too")? It seems to me that modern culture already provides too many impediments to critical thinking for us to add more.

Is it possible to carry this plain language commitment too far? Yes, and some will think I have done so in avoiding the term *inferences* and speaking instead of conclusions. But I respectfully disagree. Lexicographers point out that the distinction between these terms is extremely subtle, so it seems more reasonable not to devote time to it. Also, I avoid using the term *values* whenever possible for a somewhat different reason. The word *value* is so associated with relativism that its use in this context can undermine the crucial idea that arguments differ in quality. For many students, the word *value* triggers the thought, "Everyone has a right to his or her values; mine are right for me, and though they may need 'clarification' from time to time, they are never to be questioned." This thought impedes critical thinking.

Acknowledgments

I wish to express my appreciation to all those who contributed to the preparation of this edition. Special thanks to those who reviewed the manuscript:

Anna Villegas, *San Joaquin Delta College;*
Aimee Bissonette, *Inver Hills Community College;*
James Kruser, *Alfred State College;*
Sue Crowson, *Del Mar College;*
Erin Murphy, *University of Kentucky;*
Adrian Patten, *University of Cincinnati;*
Dedaimia Storrs Whitney, *Franklin College;*
Lisa Weisman-Davlantes, *California State–Fullerton;*
Geoffrey Phillip Bellah, *Orange Coast College;*
Karen Hoffman, *Hood College;*

xii PRFACE

Aimee Ross-Kilroy, *Loyola Marymount University;*
Deanna Davis, *College of the Canyons*

I am also grateful to John Augustine, Delta College; Lori Ebert, International Institute of the Americas; John Garcia, Cerro Coso Community College; Michael Small, Shasta College; Joel Brouwer, Montcalm Community College; Cynthia Gobatie, Riverside Community College; Anne Benvennti, Cerro Coso College; Fred Heifner Jr., Cumberland University; and Phyllis Toy, University of Southern Indiana.

PART ONE

The Context

Anyone who wishes to master an activity must first understand its tools and rules. This is as true of critical thinking as it is of golf, carpentry, flying a plane, or brain surgery. In critical thinking, however, the tools are not material objects but concepts, and the rules govern mental rather than physical performance.

This first section explores seven important concepts—*individuality, critical thinking, truth, knowledge, opinion, evidence,* and *argument*—with a chapter devoted to each. Most of these concepts are so familiar that you may be inclined to wonder whether there is any point to examining them. The answer is yes, for three reasons. First, much of what is commonly believed about these concepts is mistaken. Second, whoever examines them carefully is always rewarded with fresh insights. Third, the more thorough your knowledge of these concepts, the more proficient you will be in your thinking.

CHAPTER 1

Who Are You?

Suppose someone asked, "Who are you?" It would be simple enough to respond with your name. But if the person wanted to know the entire story about who you are, the question would be more difficult to answer. You'd obviously have to give the details of your height, age, and weight. You'd also have to include all your sentiments and preferences, even the secret ones you've never shared with anyone—your affection for your loved ones; your desire to please the people you associate with; your dislike of your older sister's husband; your allegiance to your favorite beverage, brand of clothing, and music.

Your attitudes couldn't be overlooked either—your impatience when an issue gets complex, your aversion to certain courses, your fear of high places and dogs and speaking in public. The list would go on. To be complete, it would have to include all your characteristics—not only the physical but also the emotional and intellectual.

To provide all that information would be quite a chore. But suppose the questioner was still curious and asked, "How did you get the way you are?" If your patience were not yet exhausted, chances are you'd answer something like this: "I'm this way because I choose to be, because I've considered other sentiments and preferences and attitudes and have made my selections. The ones I have chosen fit my style and personality best." That answer is natural enough, and in part it's true. But in a larger sense, it's not true. The impact of the world on all of us is much greater than most of us realize.

The Influence of Time and Place

Not only are you a member of a particular species, *Homo sapiens*, but you also exist at a particular time in the history of that species and in a particular place on the planet. That time and place are defined by specific circumstances, understandings, beliefs, and customs, all of which limit your experience and influence your thought patterns. If you had lived in America in colonial times, you likely would have had no objection to the practice of barring women from serving on a jury, entering into a legal contract, owning property, or voting. If you had lived in the nineteenth century, you would have had no objection to young children being denied an education and being hired out by their parents to work sixteen hours a day, nor would you have given any thought to the special needs of adolescence. (The concept of adolescence was not invented until 1904.)[1]

If you had been raised in the Middle East, you would stand much closer to people you converse with than you do in America. If you had been raised in India, you might be perfectly comfortable having your parents choose your spouse for you. If your native language were Spanish and your knowledge of English modest, you probably would be confused by some English colloquialisms. James Henslin offers two amusing examples of such confusion: Chevrolet Novas initially sold very poorly in Mexico because *no va* in Spanish means "it doesn't work"; and Perdue chickens were regarded with a certain suspicion (or worse) because the company's slogan—"It takes a tough man to make a tender chicken"—became in Spanish "It takes an aroused man to make a chicken affectionate."[2]

People who grow up in Europe, Asia, or South America have very different ideas of punctuality. As Daniel Goleman explains, "Five minutes is late but permissible for a business appointment in the U.S., but thirty minutes is normal in Arab countries. In England five to fifteen minutes is the 'correct' lateness for one invited to dinner; an Italian might come two hours late, an Ethiopian still later, a Javanese not at all, having accepted only to prevent his host's losing face."[3] A different ethnic origin would also mean different tastes in food. Instead of craving a New York Strip steak and french fries, you might crave "raw monkey brains" or "camel's milk cheese patties cured in dry camel's dung" and washed down with "warm camel's blood."[4] Sociologist Ian Robertson summed up the range of global dietary differences succinctly: "Americans eat oysters but not snails. The French eat snails but not locusts. The Zulus eat locusts but not fish. The Jews eat fish but not pork. The Hindus eat pork but not beef. The Russians eat beef but not snakes. The Chinese eat snakes but not people. The Jalé of New Guinea find people delicious."[5] [Note: The reference to Hindus is mistaken.]

To sum up, living in a different age or culture would make you a different person. Even if you rebelled against the values of your time and place, they still would represent the context of your life—in other words, they still would influence your responses.

The Influence of Ideas[6]

When one idea is expressed, closely related ideas are simultaneously conveyed, logically and inescapably.[7] In logic, this kinship is expressed by the term *sequitur,* Latin for "it follows." (The converse is *non sequitur,* "it does not follow.")[8]

Consider, for example, the idea that many teachers and parents express to young children as a way of encouraging them: "If you believe in yourself, you can succeed at anything." From this it follows that *nothing else* but belief—neither talent nor hard work—is necessary for success. The reason the two ideas are equivalent is that their meanings are inseparably linked.*

In addition to conveying ideas closely linked to it in meaning, an idea can *imply* other ideas. For example, the idea that there is no real difference between virtue and vice implies that people should not feel bound by common moral standards. Samuel Johnson had this implication in mind when he said: "But if he does really think that there is no distinction between virtue and vice, why, Sir, when he leaves our houses let us count our spoons."

If we were fully aware of the closely linked meanings and implications of the ideas we encounter, we could easily sort out the sound ones from the unsound, the wise from the foolish, and the helpful from the harmful. But we are seldom fully aware. In many cases, we take ideas at face value and embrace them with little or no thought of their associated meanings and implications. In the course of time, our actions are shaped by those meanings and implications, whether we are aware of them or not.

To appreciate the influence of ideas in people's lives, consider the series of events set in motion by an idea that was popular in psychology more than a century ago and whose influence continues to this day—the idea that "intelligence is genetically determined and cannot be increased."

That idea led researchers to devise tests that measure intelligence. The most famous (badly flawed) test determined that the average mental age of white American adults was 13 and that, among immigrants, the average Russian's mental age was 11.34; the average Italian's, 11.01; the average Pole's, 10.74; and the average mental age of "Negroes," 10.41.

Educators read the text results and thought, "Attempts to raise students' intelligence are pointless," so they replaced academic curricula with vocational curricula and embraced a methodology that taught students facts but not the process of judgment.

---

*The statement "Belief in oneself is an important element in success" is very different because it specifies that belief is not the only element in success.

Legislators read the test results and decided "We've got to do something to keep intellectually inferior people from entering the country," so they revised immigration laws to discriminate against southern and central Europeans.

Eugenicists, who had long been concerned about the welfare of the human species, saw the tests as a grave warning. They thought, "If intelligence cannot be increased, we must find ways of encouraging reproduction among people of higher intelligence and discouraging it among those of lower intelligence."

The eugenicists' concern inspired a variety of actions. Margaret Sanger's Planned Parenthood urged the lower classes to practice contraception. Others succeeded in legalizing promoted forced sterilization, notably in Virginia. The U.S. Supreme Court upheld the Virginia law with Justice Oliver Wendell Holmes, Jr. declaring, "Three generations of imbeciles are enough."[9] Over the next five decades 7,500 women, including "unwed mothers, prostitutes, petty criminals and children with disciplinary problems" were sterilized.[10] In addition, by 1950 over 150,000 supposedly "defective" children, many relatively normal, were held against their will in institutions. They "endured isolation, overcrowding, forced labor, and physical abuse including lobotomy, electroshock, and surgical sterilization."[11]

Meanwhile, business leaders read the test results and decided, *"We need policies to ensure that workers leave their minds at the factory gate and perform their assigned tasks mindlessly."* So they enacted those policies. Decades later, when Edwards Deming proposed his "quality control" ideas for involving workers in decision making, business leaders remembered those test results and ignored Deming's advice. (In contrast, the Japanese welcomed Deming's ideas; as a result, several of their industries surged ahead of their American competition.)

These are the most obvious effects of hereditarianism but they are certainly not the only ones. Others include discrimination against racial and ethnic minorities and the often-paternalistic policies of government offered in response. (Some historians also link hereditarianism to the genocide that occurred in Nazi Germany.)

The innumerable ideas you have encountered will affect your beliefs and behavior in similar ways—sometimes slightly, at other times profoundly. And this can happen even if you have not consciously embraced the ideas.

The Influence of Mass Culture

In centuries past, family and teachers were the dominant, and sometimes the only, influence on children. Today, however, the influence exerted by mass culture (the broadcast media, newspapers, magazines, Internet and popular music) often is greater.

By age 18 the average teenager has spent 11,000 hours in the classroom and 22,000 hours in front of the television set. He or she has had perhaps 13,000 school lessons yet has watched more than 750,000 commercials. By age thirty-five the same person has had fewer than 20,000 school lessons yet has watched approximately 45,000 hours of television and close to 2 million commercials.

What effects does mass culture have on us? To answer, we need only consider the formats and devices commonly used in the media. Modern advertising typically bombards the public with slogans and testimonials by celebrities. This approach is designed to appeal to emotions and create artificial needs for products and services. As a result, many people develop the habit of responding emotionally, impulsively, and gullibly to such appeals. They also tend to acquire values very different from those taught in the home and the school. Ads often portray play as more fulfilling than work, self-gratification as more desirable than self-control, and materialism as more meaningful than idealism.

Television programmers use frequent scene shifts and sensory appeals such as car crashes, violence, and sexual encounters to keep audience interest from diminishing. Then they add frequent commercial interruptions. This author has analyzed the attention shifts that television viewers are subjected to. In a dramatic program, for example, attention shifts might include camera angle changes;* shifts in story line from one set of characters (or subplot) to another, or from a present scene to a past scene (flashback), or to fantasy; and shifts to "newsbreaks," to commercial breaks, from one commercial to another, and back to the program. Also included might be shifts of attention that occur within commercials. I found as many as 78 shifts per hour, excluding the shifts within commercials. The number of shifts within commercials ranged from 6 to 54 and averaged approximately 17 per fifteen-second commercial. The total number of attention shifts came out to over 800 per hour, or over 14 per minute.†

This manipulation has prevented many people from developing a mature attention span. They expect the classroom and the workplace to provide the same constant excitement they get from television. That, of course, is an impossible demand, and when it isn't met they call their teachers boring and their work unfulfilling. Because such people seldom have the patience to read books that require them to think, many publishers have replaced serious books with light fare written by celebrities.

Even when writers of serious books do manage to become published authors, they are often directed to give short, dramatic answers during promotional interviews, sometimes at the expense of accuracy. A man who coaches writers for talk shows offered one client this advice: "If I ask you whether the budget deficit is a good thing or a bad thing, you should not say, 'Well, it stimulates the economy but it passes on a burden.' You

---

*This is typically accomplished by using two or more cameras and switching from one camera to another.
†There are about eleven minutes of commercials per hour, the exact time varying by network and program. Thus, at a rate of 4 per minute, the total number of commercials per hour is 44. This calculates, therefore, to 78 shifts outside commercials plus 748 shifts (17 shifts per commercial × 44 commercials per hour) within commercials for a total of 826.

have to say 'It's a great idea!' or 'It's a terrible idea!' It doesn't matter which."[12] (*Translation*: "Don't give a balanced answer. Give an oversimplified one because it will get you noticed.")

Print journalism is also in the grip of sensationalism. As a newspaper editor observed, "Journalists keep trying to find people who are at 1 or at 9 on a scale of 1 to 10 rather than people at 3 to 7 [the more moderate positions] where most people actually are."[13] Another journalist claims, "News is now becoming more opinion than verified fact. Journalists are slipping into entertainment rather than telling us the verified facts we need to know."[14]

Today's politicians often manipulate people more offensively than do journalists. Instead of expressing their thoughts, some politicians find out what people think and pretend to share their ideas. Many politicians hire people to conduct polls and focus groups to learn what messages will "sell." They even go so far as to test the impact of certain words—that is why we hear so much about "trust," "family," "character," and "values" these days. Political science professor Larry Sabato says that during the Clinton impeachment trial, the president's advisors used the term *private lives* over and over—James Carville used it six times in one four-minute speech—because they knew it could persuade people into believing the president's lying under oath was of no great consequence.[15]

The "Science" of Manipulation

Attempts to influence the thoughts and actions of others are no doubt as old as time, but manipulation did not become a science until the early twentieth century, when Ivan Pavlov, a Russian professor of psychology, published his research on conditioned (learned) reflexes. Pavlov found that by ringing a bell when he fed a dog, he could condition the dog to drool at the sound of the bell even when no food was presented. An American psychologist, John Watson, was impressed with Pavlov's findings and applied them to human behavior. In Watson's most famous experiment, he let a baby touch a laboratory rat. At first, the baby was unafraid. But then Watson hit a hammer against metal whenever the baby reached out to touch the rat, and the baby became frightened and cried. In time, the baby cried not only at the sight of the rat but also at the sight of anything furry, such as a stuffed animal.* Watson's work earned him the title "father of behaviorism."

Less well known is Watson's application of behaviorist principles to advertising. He spent the latter part of his career working for advertising agencies and soon recognized that the most effective appeal to consumers

*Modern ethical norms would not allow a child to be used in such an experiment.

was not to the mind but to the emotions. He advised advertisers to "tell [the consumer] something that will tie him up with fear, something that will stir up a mild rage, that will call out an affectionate or love response, or strike at a deep psychological or habit need." His attitude toward the consumer is perhaps best indicated by a statement he made in a presentation to department store executives: "The consumer is to the manufacturer, the department stores and the advertising agencies, what the green frog is to the physiologist."[16]

Watson introduced these strategies in the 1920s and 1930s, the age of newspapers and radio. Since the advent of television, these advertising strategies have grown more sophisticated and effective, so much so that many individuals and groups with political and social agendas have adopted them. The strategies work for a number of reasons, the chief one being people's conviction that they are impervious to manipulation. This belief is mistaken, as many researchers have demonstrated. For example, Solomon Asch showed that people's reactions can be altered simply by changing the order of words in a series. He asked study participants to evaluate a person by a series of adjectives. When he put positive adjectives first—"intelligent, industrious, impulsive, critical, stubborn, envious"— the participants gave a positive evaluation. When he reversed the order, with "envious" coming first and "intelligent" last, they gave a negative evaluation.[17]

Similarly, research has shown that human memory can be manipulated. The way a question is asked can change the details in a person's memory and even make a person *remember something that never happened*![18]

Of course, advertisers and people with political or social agendas are not content to stimulate emotions and/or plant ideas in our minds. They also seek to reinforce those impressions by repeating them again and again. The more people hear a slogan or talking point, the more familiar it becomes. Before long, it becomes indistinguishable from ideas developed through careful thought. Sadly, "the packaging is often done so effectively that the viewer, listener, or reader does not make up his own mind at all. Instead, he inserts a packaged opinion into his mind, somewhat like inserting a DVD into a DVD player. He then pushes a button and 'plays back' the opinion whenever it seems appropriate to do so. He has performed acceptably without having had to think."[19] Many of the beliefs we hold dearest and defend most vigorously may have been planted in our minds in just this way.

Many years ago, Harry A. Overstreet noted that "a climate of opinion, like a physical climate, is so pervasive a thing that those who live within it and know no other take it for granted."[20] The rise of mass culture and the sophisticated use of manipulation have made this insight more relevant today than ever.

The Influence of Psychology

The social and psychological theories of our time also have an impact on our beliefs. Before the past few decades, people were urged to be self-disciplined, self-critical, and self-effacing. They were urged to practice self-denial, to aspire to self-knowledge, to behave in a manner that ensured they maintained self-respect. Self-centeredness was considered a vice. "Hard work," they were told, "leads to achievement, and that in turn produces satisfaction and self-confidence." By and large, our grandparents internalized those teachings. When they honored them in their behavior, they felt proud; when they dishonored them, they felt ashamed.

Today the theories have been changed—indeed, almost exactly reversed. Self-esteem, which nineteenth-century satirist Ambrose Bierce defined as "an erroneous appraisement," is now considered an imperative. Self-centeredness has been transformed from vice into virtue, and people who devote their lives to helping others, people once considered heroic and saintlike, are now said to be afflicted with "a disease to please." The formula for success and happiness begins with feeling good about ourselves. Students who do poorly in school, workers who don't measure up to the challenges of their jobs, substance abusers, lawbreakers—all are typically diagnosed as deficient in self-esteem.

In addition, just as our grandparents internalized the social and psychological theories of their time, so most contemporary Americans have internalized the message of self-esteem. We hear people speak of it over coffee; we hear it endlessly invoked on talk shows. Challenges to its precepts are usually met with disapproval.

But isn't the theory of self-esteem self-evident? No. A negative perception of our abilities will, of course, handicap our performance. Dr. Maxwell Maltz explains the amazing results one educator had in improving the grades of schoolchildren by changing their self-images. The educator had observed that when the children saw themselves as stupid in a particular subject (or stupid in general), they unconsciously acted to confirm their self-images. They believed they were stupid, so they acted that way. Reasoning that it was their defeatist attitude rather than any lack of ability that was undermining their efforts, the educator set out to change their self-images. He found that when he accomplished that, *they no longer behaved stupidly*! Maltz concludes from this and other examples that our experiences can work a kind of self-hypnotism on us, suggesting a conclusion about ourselves and then urging us to make it come true.[21]

Many proponents of self-esteem went far beyond Maltz's demonstration that self-confidence is an important ingredient in success. They claimed that there is no such thing as too much self-esteem. Research does not support that claim. For example, Martin Seligman, an eminent research psychologist and founder of the movement known as positive psychology, cites significant evidence that, rather than *solving* personal and social problems, including depression, the modern emphasis on self-esteem *causes* them.[22]

Maltz's research documents that lack of confidence impedes performance, a valuable insight. But such research doesn't explain why the more global concept of self-esteem has become so dominant. The answer to that question lies in the popularization of the work of humanistic psychologists such as Abraham Maslow. Maslow described what he called the hierarchy of human needs in the form of a pyramid, with physiological needs (food and drink) at the foundation. Above them, in ascending order, are safety needs, the need for belongingness and love, the need for esteem and approval, and aesthetic and cognitive needs (knowledge, understanding, etc.). At the pinnacle is the need for self-actualization, or fulfillment of our potential. In Maslow's view, the lower needs must be fulfilled before the higher ones. It's easy to see how the idea that self-esteem must precede achievement was derived from Maslow's theory.

Other theories might have been adopted, however. A notable one is Austrian psychiatrist Viktor Frankl's, which was advanced at roughly the same time as Maslow's and was based on both Frankl's professional practice and his experiences in Hitler's concentration camps. Frankl argues that one human need is higher than self-actualization: *self-transcendence*, the need to rise above narrow absorption with self. According to Frankl, "the primordial anthropological fact [is] that being human is being always directed, and pointing to something or someone other than oneself: to a meaning to fulfill or another human being to encounter, a cause to serve or a person to love." A person becomes fully human "by forgetting himself and giving himself, overlooking himself and focusing outward."

Making self-actualization (or happiness) the direct object of our pursuit, in Frankl's view, is ultimately self-defeating; such fulfillment can occur only as "the unintended effect of self-transcendence."[23] The proper perspective on life, Frankl believes, is not what it can give *to* us, but what it expects *from* us; life is daily—even hourly—questioning us, challenging us to accept "the responsibility to find the right answer to its problems and to fulfill the tasks which it constantly sets for [each of us]."[24]

Finding meaning, according to Frankl's theory, involves "perceiving a possibility embedded in reality" and searching for challenging tasks "whose completion might add meaning to [one's] existence." But such perceiving and searching are frustrated by the focus on self: "As long as modern literature confines itself to, and contents itself with, self-expression—not to say self-exhibition—it reflects its authors' sense of futility and absurdity. What is more important, it also creates absurdity. This is understandable in light of the fact that meaning must be discovered, it cannot be invented. Sense cannot be created, but what may well be created is nonsense."[25]

Whether we agree completely with Frankl, one thing is clear: Contemporary American culture would be markedly different if the emphasis over the past several decades had been on Frankl's theory rather than on the theories of Maslow and the other humanistic psychologists. All of us would have been affected—we can only imagine how profoundly—in our attitudes, values, and beliefs.

Becoming an Individual

In light of what we have discussed, we should regard individuality not as something we are born with but rather as something acquired—or, more precisely, *earned.* Individuality begins in the realization that it is impossible to escape being influenced by other people and by circumstance. The essence of individuality is vigilance. The following guidelines will help you achieve this:

1. *Treat your first reaction to any person, issue, or situation as tentative.* No matter how appealing it may be, refuse to embrace it until you have examined it.
2. *Decide why you reacted as you did.* Consider whether you borrowed the reaction from someone else—a parent or friend, perhaps, or a celebrity or fictional character on television. If possible, determine what specific experiences conditioned you to react this way.
3. *Think of other possible reactions you might have had to the person, issue, or situation.*
4. *Ask yourself whether one of the other reactions is more appropriate than your first reaction.* And when you answer, resist the influence of your conditioning.

To ensure that you will really be an individual and not merely claim to be one, apply these guidelines throughout your work in this book, as well as in your everyday life.

Applications

Note: One of the best ways to develop your thinking (and writing) skills is to record your observations, questions, and ideas in a journal and then, as time permits, to reflect on what you have recorded—considering the meaning and application of the observations, answering the questions, elaborating on the ideas (and, where appropriate, challenging them), and recording your insights. An inexpensive bound notebook or spiral notebook will serve the purpose. A good approach is to record your initial observations, questions, and ideas on the left side of the page, leaving the right side blank for your later analysis and commentary. The value of this reflective process is so great that you should consider keeping such a journal even if your instructor does not make it a formal part of the course.

1. Do a brief study of attention shifts such as the one described in the chapter. Record a half-hour show. Then play the show back twice, the first time counting the number of shifts within the program, excluding commercials, and the second time counting only those within commercials. Complete the necessary arithmetic and be prepared to share your results in class.

2. Reflect on your findings in application 1. Write several paragraphs discussing the implications of those findings for education, business, and family life.

3. Many people cheerfully pay $6 or $7 a gallon for designer drinking water but moan and groan when they have to pay $3 a gallon for gasoline. Does anything you read in this chapter help you understand why this is so?

4. Imagine how different America might be if Frankl's emphasis on self-transcendence and personal responsibility, rather than Maslow's emphasis on self-actualization and popular culture's emphasis on self-esteem, had been dominant for the past fifty years. List as many ways as you can in which our society might be different today and comment on whether each would be beneficial or harmful. Be prepared to explain your views in class discussion.

5. Watch one of the music video channels—MTV, VH1, CMT, BET— for at least an hour. Analyze how men and women are depicted in the videos. Note significant details. For example, observe whether men are depicted in power roles more than women and whether women are portrayed as objects of male desire. Decide what attitudes and values are conveyed. (You might want to record as you are watching so that you can review what you have seen, freeze significant frames for closer analysis, and keep your observations for later reference or class viewing and discussion.)

6. Suppose you asked a friend, "How did you acquire your particular identity—your sentiments and preferences and attitudes?" Then suppose the friend responded, "I'm an individual. No one else influences me. I do my own thing, and I select the sentiments and preferences and attitudes that suit me." How would you explain to your friend what you learned in this chapter?

7. Ask yourself the question, Who am I? Write down ten answers to this question, each on a separate slip of paper. Use the first three paragraphs of this chapter to help you frame your answers. Arrange the pieces of paper in order of their importance to you. Then explain the arrangement—that is, which self-descriptions are most important to you, and why?

8. Identify the various positive and negative influences that have shaped you. Be sure to include the particular as well as the general and the subtle as well as the obvious influences. Which of those influences have had the greatest effect on you? Explain the effects as precisely as you can.

9. Note your immediate reaction to each of the following statements. Then apply the four guidelines given in this chapter for achieving individuality.
   a. Health care workers should be required to be tested for HIV/AIDS.
   b. Beauty contests and talent competitions for children should be banned.
   c. Extremist groups like the Ku Klux Klan should be allowed to hold rallies on public property or be issued permits to hold parades on city streets.
   d. Freshman composition should be a required course for all students.
   e. High school and college athletes should be tested for anabolic steroid use.
   f. Creationism should be taught in high school biology classes.

g. Polygamy should be legalized.

h. The voting age should be lowered to sixteen.

i. The prison system should give greater emphasis to the punishment of inmates than to their rehabilitation.

j. Doctors and clinics should be required to notify parents of minors when they prescribe birth control devices or facilitate abortions for the minors.

k. A man's self-esteem is severely injured if his wife makes more money than he makes.

l. Women like being dependent on men.

10. *Group discussion exercise:* Discuss several of the statements in application 9 with two or three of your classmates, applying the four guidelines presented in this chapter for developing individuality. Be prepared to share your group's ideas with the class.

A Difference of Opinion

The following passage summarizes an important difference of opinion. After reading the statement, use the library and/or the Internet and find what knowledgeable people have said about the issue. Be sure to cover the entire range of views. Then assess the strengths and weaknesses of each. If you conclude that one view is entirely correct and the others are mistaken, explain how you reached that conclusion. If, *as is more likely,* you find that one view is more insightful than the others but that they all make some valid points, construct a view of your own that *combines* insights from all views and explain why that view is the most reasonable of all. Present your response in a composition or an oral report, as your instructor specifies.

Should captured terrorists be tried in military or criminal courts? When the United States decided to use the military base at Guantanamo Bay, Cuba, to detain individuals captured on the battlefield in the Iraq war, many people protested the decision. Some argued that captured individuals should be considered criminals rather than prisoners of war and accorded the rights guaranteed by the U.S. Constitution to all people accused of crimes. Others argued for classifying the individuals as prisoners of war and treating them as specified in the Geneva Conventions of 1949. Supporters of the government's decision reject both arguments, contending that captured terrorists are neither criminals nor soldiers but "unlawful combatants," adding that any other designation would impose burdens on the United States that would make it difficult to fight terrorism and thereby threaten national security.

Begin your analysis by conducting a Google search using the term "status captured terrorists."

CHAPTER 2

What Is Critical Thinking?

When Arthur was in the first grade, the teacher directed the class to "think." "Now, class," she said, "I know this problem is a little harder than the ones we've been doing, but I'm going to give you a few extra minutes to think about it. Now start thinking."

It was not the first time Arthur had heard the word used. He'd heard it many times at home, but never quite this way. The teacher seemed to be asking for some special activity, something he should know how to start and stop—like his father's car. "Vroom-m-m," he muttered half aloud. Because of his confusion, he was unaware he was making the noise.

"Arthur, please stop making noises and start thinking."

Embarrassed and not knowing quite what to do, he looked down at his desk. Then, out of the corner of his eye, he noticed that the little girl next to him was staring at the ceiling. "Maybe that's the way you start thinking," he guessed. He decided the others had probably learned how to do it last year, that time he was home with the measles. So he stared at the ceiling.

As he progressed through grade school and high school, he heard that same direction hundreds of times. "No, that's not the answer, you're not thinking—now *think!*" And occasionally he would hear from particularly self-pitying teachers given to muttering to themselves aloud: "What did I do to deserve this? Don't they teach them anything in the grades anymore? Don't you people care about ideas? Think, dammit, THINK."

So Arthur learned to feel somewhat guilty about the whole matter. Obviously, this thinking was an important activity that he'd failed to learn. Maybe he lacked the brain power. But he was resourceful enough. He watched the other students and did what they did. Whenever a teacher started in about thinking, he screwed up his face, furrowed his brow, scratched his head, stroked his chin, stared off into space or up at the ceiling, and repeated silently to himself, "Let's see now, I've got to think about that, think, think—I hope he doesn't call on me—think."

16

Though Arthur didn't know it, that's just what the other students were saying to themselves.

Your experience may have been similar to Arthur's. In other words, many people may have simply told you to think without ever explaining what thinking is and what qualities a good thinker has that a poor thinker lacks. If that is the case, you have a lot of company. Extensive, effective training in thinking is the exception rather than the rule. This fact and its unfortunate consequences are suggested by the following comments from accomplished observers of the human condition:

> The most interesting and astounding contradiction in life is to me the constant insistence by nearly all people upon "logic," "logical reasoning," "sound reasoning," on the one hand, and on the other their inability to display it, and their unwillingness to accept it when displayed by others.[1]

> Most of our so-called reasoning consists in finding arguments for going on believing as we already do.[2]

> Clear thinking is a very rare thing, but even just plain thinking is almost as rare. Most of us most of the time do not think at all. We believe and we feel, but we do not think.[3]

> Mental indolence is one of the commonest of human traits.[4]

[handwritten margin note: What thinking is actually...]

What is this activity that everyone claims is important but few people have mastered? Thinking is a general term used to cover numerous activities, from daydreaming to reflection and analysis. Here are just some of the synonyms listed in *Roget's Thesaurus* for *think*:

appreciate ✓	consult ✓	fancy	reason ✓
believe ✓	contemplate ✓	imagine ✓	reflect ✓
cerebrate	deliberate	meditate	ruminate
cogitate	digest	muse ✓	speculate ✓
conceive	discuss ✓	ponder ✓	suppose ✓
consider ✓	dream ✓	realize ✓	weigh

All of those are just the *names* that thinking goes under. They really don't explain it. The fact is, after thousands of years of humans' experiencing thought and talking and writing about thinking, it remains in many respects one of the great mysteries of our existence. Still, though much is yet to be learned, a great deal is already known.

Mind, Brain, or Both?

Most modern researchers use the word *mind* synonymously with *brain*, as if the physical organ that resides in the human skull were solely responsible for thinking. This practice conveniently presupposes that a problem that has challenged the greatest thinkers for millennia—the relationship between mind and physical matter—was somehow solved when no one was looking. The problem itself and the individuals who spent their lives wrestling with it deserve better.

Neuroscience has provided a number of valuable insights into the cognitive or thinking activities of the brain. It has documented that the left hemisphere of the brain deals mainly with detailed language processing and is associated with analysis and logical thinking, that the right hemisphere deals mainly with sensory images and is associated with intuition and creative thinking, and that the small bundle of nerves that lies between the hemispheres—the corpus callosum—integrates the various functions.

The research that produced these insights showed that the brain is *necessary* for thought, but it has not shown that the brain is *sufficient* for thought. In fact, many philosophers claim it can never show that. They argue that the mind and the brain are demonstrably different. Whereas the brain is a *physical* entity composed of matter and therefore subject to decay, the mind is a *metaphysical* entity. Examine brain cells under the most powerful microscope and you will never see an idea or concept— for example, beauty, government, equality, or love—because ideas and concepts are not material entities and so have no physical dimension. Where, then, do these nonmaterial things reside? In the nonmaterial mind.[5]

The late American philosopher William Barrett observed that "history is, fundamentally, the adventure of human consciousness" and "the fundamental history of humankind is the history of mind." In his view, "one of the supreme ironies of modern history" is the fact that science, which owes its very existence to the human mind, has had the audacity to deny the reality of the mind. As he put it, "the offspring denies the parent."[6]

The argument over whether the mind is a reality is not the only issue about the mind that has been hotly debated over the centuries. One especially important issue is whether the mind is *passive*, a blank slate on which experience writes, as John Locke held, or *active*, a vehicle by which we take the initiative and exercise our free will, as G. W. Leibnitz argued. This book is based on the latter view.

Critical Thinking Defined

Let's begin by making the important distinction between thinking and feeling. *I feel* and *I think* are sometimes used interchangeably, but that practice causes confusion. Feeling is a subjective response that reflects emotion, sentiment, or desire; it generally occurs spontaneously rather than through a conscious mental act. We don't have to employ our minds to feel angry when we are insulted, afraid when we are threatened, or compassionate when we see a picture of a starving child. The feelings arise automatically.

Feeling is useful in directing our attention to matters we should think about; it also can provide the enthusiasm and commitment necessary to complete arduous mental tasks. However, feeling is never a good substitute for thinking because it is notoriously unreliable. Some feelings are beneficial, honorable, even noble; others are not, as everyday experience demonstrates. We often feel like doing things that will harm us—for example, smoking, sunbathing without sunscreen, telling off our professor or employer, or spending the rent money on lottery tickets.

Zinedine Zidane was one of the greatest soccer players of his generation, and many experts believed that in his final season (2006) he would lead France to the pinnacle of soccer success—winning the coveted World Cup. But then, toward the end of the championship game against Italy, he viciously head-butted an Italian player in full view of hundreds of millions of people. The referee banished him from the field, France lost the match, and *a single surrender to feeling* forever stained the brilliant career Zidane had dedicated his life to building.

In contrast to feeling, thinking is a conscious mental process performed to solve a problem, make a decision, or gain understanding.* Whereas feeling has no purpose beyond expressing itself, thinking aims beyond itself to knowledge or action. This is not to say that thinking is infallible; in fact, a good part of this book is devoted to exposing errors in thinking and showing you how to avoid them. Yet for all its shortcomings, thinking is the most reliable guide to action we humans possess. To sum up the relationship between feeling and thinking, feelings need to be tested before being trusted, and thinking is the most reasonable and reliable way to test them.

There are three broad categories of thinking: reflective, creative, and critical. The focus of this book is on critical thinking. The essence of critical thinking is *evaluation*. Critical thinking, therefore, may be defined as the process by which we test claims and arguments and determine which have merit and which do not. In other words, critical thinking is a search for answers, a *quest*. Not surprisingly, one of the most important techniques used in critical thinking is asking probing *questions*. Where the uncritical accept their first thoughts and other people's statements at face value, critical thinkers challenge all ideas in this manner:

---

*Some informal definitions of thinking include daydreaming. It is excluded from this definition because daydreaming is a passive mental state over which we exercise little or no control. It is therefore of little use in evaluating ideas.

Thought	*Question*
Professor Vile cheated me in my composition grade. He weighted some themes more heavily than others.	Did he grade everyone on the same standard? Were the different weightings justified?
Before women entered the work force, there were fewer divorces. That shows that a woman's place is in the home.	How do you know that this factor, and not some other one(s), is responsible for the increase in divorces?
A college education isn't worth what you pay for it. Some people never reach a salary level appreciably higher than the level they would have reached without the degree.	Is money the only measure of the worth of an education? What about increased understanding of self and life and increased ability to cope with challenges?

Critical thinking also employs questions to analyze issues. Consider, for example, the subject of values. When it is being discussed, some people say, "Our country has lost its traditional values" and "There would be less crime, especially violent crime, if parents and teachers emphasized moral values." Critical thinking would prompt us to ask,

1. What is the relationship between values and beliefs? Between values and convictions?
2. Are all values *valuable*?
3. How aware is the average person of his or her values? Is it possible that many people deceive themselves about their real values?
4. Where do one's values originate? Within the individual or outside? In thought or in feeling?
5. Does education change a person's values? If so, is this change always for the better?
6. Should parents and teachers attempt to shape children's values?

Characteristics of Critical Thinkers

A number of misconceptions exist about critical thinking. One is that being able to support beliefs with reasons makes one a critical thinker. Virtually everyone has reasons, however weak they may be. The test of critical thinking is whether the reasons are good and sufficient.

Another misconception is that critical thinkers never imitate others in thought or action. If that were the case, then every eccentric would be a critical thinker. Critical thinking means making sound decisions, regardless of how common or uncommon those decisions are.

Critical thinking

misconceptions

It is also a misconception that critical thinking is synonymous with having a lot of right answers in one's head. There's nothing wrong with having right answers, of course. But critical thinking involves the process of finding answers when they are not so readily available.

And yet another misconception is that critical thinking cannot be learned, that one either has it or does not. On the contrary, critical thinking is a matter of habit. The most careless, sloppy thinker can become a critical thinker by developing the characteristics of a critical thinker. This is not to say that all people have equal thinking potential but rather that everyone can achieve dramatic improvement.

We have already noted one characteristic of critical thinkers—skill in asking appropriate questions. Another is control of one's mental activities. John Dewey once observed that more of our time than most of us care to admit is spent "trifling with mental pictures, random recollections, pleasant but unfounded hopes, flitting, half-developed impressions."[7] Good thinkers are no exception. However, they have learned better than poor thinkers how to stop that casual, semiconscious drift of images when they wish and how to fix their minds on one specific matter, examine it carefully, and form a judgment about it. They have learned, in other words, how to take charge of their thoughts, to use their minds actively as well as passively.

Here are some additional characteristics of critical thinkers, as contrasted with those of uncritical thinkers:

Critical Thinkers . . .	*Uncritical Thinkers . . .*
Are honest with themselves, acknowledging what they don't know, recognizing their limitations, and being watchful of their own errors.	Pretend they know more than they do, ignore their limitations, and assume their views are error-free.
Regard problems and controversial issues as exciting challenges.	Regard problems and controversial issues as nuisances or threats to their ego.
Strive for understanding, keep curiosity alive, remain patient with complexity, and are ready to invest time to overcome confusion.	Are impatient with complexity and thus would rather remain confused than make the effort to understand.
Base judgments on evidence rather than personal preferences, deferring judgment whenever evidence is insufficient. They revise judgments when new evidence reveals error.	Base judgments on first impressions and gut reactions. They are unconcerned about the amount or quality of evidence and cling to their views steadfastly.

Are interested in other people's ideas and so are willing to read and listen attentively, even when they tend to disagree with the other person.	Are preoccupied with themselves and their own opinions and so are unwilling to pay attention to others' views. At the first sign of disagreement, they tend to think, "How can I refute this?"
Recognize that extreme views (whether conservative or liberal) are seldom correct, so they avoid them, practice fairmindedness, and seek a balanced view.	Ignore the need for balance and give preference to views that support their established views.
Practice restraint, controlling their feelings rather than being controlled by them, and thinking before acting.	Tend to follow their feelings and act impulsively.

As the desirable qualities suggest, critical thinking depends on mental discipline. Effective thinkers exert control over their mental life, direct their thoughts rather than being directed by them, and withhold their endorsement of any idea—even their own—until they have tested and confirmed it. John Dewey equated this mental discipline with freedom. That is, he argued that people who do not have it are not free persons but slaves to whim or circumstance:

> If a man's actions are not guided by thoughtful conclusions, then they are guided by inconsiderate impulse, unbalanced appetite, caprice, or the circumstances of the moment. To cultivate unhindered, unreflective external activity is to foster enslavement, for it leaves the person at the mercy of appetite, sense, and circumstance.[8]

The Role of Intuition

Intuition is commonly defined as immediate perception or comprehension of something—that is, sensing or understanding something without the use of reasoning. Some everyday experiences seem to support this definition. You may have met a stranger and instantly "known" that you would be partners for life. When a car salesman told you that the price he was quoting you was his final, rock-bottom price, your intuition may have told you he was lying. On the first day of a particular course, you may have had a strong sense that you would not do well in it.

Some important discoveries seem to have occurred instantaneously. For example, the German chemist Kekule found the solution to a difficult chemical problem intuitively. He was very tired when he slipped into a daydream. The image of a snake swallowing its tail came to him—and that provided the clue to the structure of the benzene molecule, which is a ring, rather than a chain, of atoms.[9] The German writer Goethe had been experiencing great difficulty organizing a large mass of material for one of his works when he learned of the tragic suicide of a close friend. At that very instant, the plan for organizing his material occurred to him in detail.[10] The English writer Samuel Taylor Coleridge (you may have read his *Rime of the Ancient Mariner* in high school) awoke from a dream with 200–300 lines of a new and complex poem clearly in mind.

Such examples seem to suggest that intuition is very different from reasoning and is not influenced by it. But before accepting that conclusion, consider these facts:

> Breakthrough ideas favor trained, active minds. It is unusual for someone totally untrained in a subject to make a significant new discovery about it. Thus, if Kekule had been a plumber, Goethe a bookkeeper, and Coleridge a hairdresser, they would almost certainly not have received the intuitions for which they are famous.

> Some intuitions eventually prove to be mistaken. That attractive stranger may turn out to be not your lifelong partner but a person for whom you develop a strong dislike. The car salesman's final price may have proved to be exactly that. And instead of doing poorly in that course, you may have done well.

> It is difficult to make an overall assessment of the quality of our intuitions because we tend to forget the ones that prove mistaken in much the same way a gambler forgets his losses.

These facts have led some scholars to conclude that intuition is simply a consequence of thinking. They would say that something about the stranger appealed to you, something the salesman said or did suggested insincerity, something about the professor frightened you. In each case, they would explain, you made a quick decision—so quick, in fact, that you were unaware that you'd been thinking. In the case of the breakthrough ideas, the scholars would say that when people become engrossed in problems or issues, their unconscious minds often continue working on them long after they have turned their attention elsewhere. Thus, when an insight seems to come "out of nowhere," it is actually a delayed result of thinking.

Which view of intuitions is the correct one? Are intuitions different from and independent of thinking or not? Perhaps, for now, the most prudent answer is that sometimes they are independent and sometimes they are not; we can't be sure when they are, and therefore it is imprudent to rely on them.

Basic Activities in Critical Thinking

The basic activities in critical thinking are investigation, interpretation, and judgment, in that order. The following chart summarizes each activity in relation to the other two.

Activity	Definition	Requirements
Investigation	Finding evidence—that is, data that will answer key questions about the issue	The evidence must be both relevant and sufficient.
Interpretation	Deciding what the evidence means	The interpretation must be more reasonable than competing interpretations.
Judgment	Reaching a conclusion about the issue	The conclusion must meet the test of logic.

As we noted previously, irresponsible thinkers first choose their conclusions and then seek out evidence to justify their choices. They fail to realize that the only conclusion worth drawing is one based on a thorough understanding of the problem or issue and its possible solutions or resolutions. Is it acceptable to speculate, guess, and form hunches and hypotheses? Absolutely. Such activities provide a helpful starting point for the thinking process. (Besides, we couldn't avoid doing so even if we tried.) The crucial thing is not to let hunches and hypotheses manipulate our thinking and dictate our conclusion in advance.

Critical Thinking and Writing

Writing may be used for either of two broad purposes: to discover ideas or to communicate them. Most of the writing you have done in school is undoubtedly the latter kind. But the former can be very helpful, not only in sorting out ideas you've already produced, but also in stimulating the flow of new ideas. For some reason, the very act of writing down one idea seems to generate additional ideas.

Whenever you write to discover ideas, focus on the issue you are examining and record all your thoughts, questions, and assertions. Don't worry about organization or correctness. If ideas come slowly, be patient. If they come suddenly, in a rush, don't try to slow down the process and develop any one of them; simply jot them all down. (There will be time for elaboration and correction later.) Direct your mind's effort, but be sensitive to ideas on the fringe of consciousness. Often they, too, will prove valuable.

If you have done your discovery writing well and have thought critically about the ideas you have produced, the task of writing to communicate will be easier and more enjoyable. You will have many more ideas—carefully evaluated ones—to develop and organize.

Critical Thinking and Discussion[11]

(handwritten: Pros + cons of discussion)

At its best, discussion deepens understanding and promotes problem solving and decision making. At its worst, it frays nerves, creates animosity, and leaves important issues unresolved. Unfortunately, the most prominent models for discussion in contemporary culture—radio and TV talk shows—often produce the latter effects.

Many hosts demand that their guests answer complex questions with simple "yes" or "no" answers. If the guests respond that way, they are attacked for oversimplifying. If, instead, they try to offer a balanced answer, the host shouts, "You're not answering the question," and proceeds to answer it himself. Guests who agree with the host are treated warmly; others are dismissed as ignorant or dishonest. Often as not, when two guests are debating, each takes a turn interrupting while the other shouts, "Let me finish." Neither shows any desire to learn from the other. Typically, as the show draws to a close, the host thanks the participants for a "vigorous debate" and promises the audience more of the same next time.

Here are some simple guidelines for ensuring that the discussions you engage in—in the classroom, on the job, or at home—are more civil, meaningful, and productive than what you see on TV. By following these guidelines, you will set a good example for the people around you.

Whenever possible, prepare in advance. Not every discussion can be prepared for in advance, but many can. An agenda is usually circulated several days before a business or committee meeting. In college courses, the assignment schedule provides a reliable indication of what will be discussed in class on a given day. Use this information to prepare: Begin by reflecting on what you already know about the topic. Then decide how you can expand your knowledge and devote some time to doing so. (Fifteen or twenty minutes of focused searching in the library or on the Internet can produce a significant amount of information on almost any subject.) Try to anticipate the different points of view that might be expressed in the discussion and consider the relative merits of each. Keep your conclusions tentative at this point, so that you will be open to the facts and interpretations others will present.

Set reasonable expectations. Have you ever left a discussion disappointed that others hadn't abandoned their views and embraced yours? Have you ever felt offended when someone disagreed with you or asked you what evidence you had to support your opinion? If the answer to either question is yes, you probably expect too much of others. People seldom change their minds easily or quickly, particularly in the case of long-held convictions.

(handwritten left margin: Steps to good discussion)

And when they encounter ideas that differ from their own, they naturally want to know what evidence supports those ideas. Expect to have your ideas questioned, and be cheerful and gracious in responding.

Leave egotism and personal agendas at the door. To be productive, discussion requires an atmosphere of mutual respect and civility. Egotism produces disrespectful attitudes toward others—notably, "I'm more important than other people," "My ideas are better than anyone else's," and "Rules don't apply to me." Personal agendas, such as dislike for another participant or excessive zeal for a point of view, can lead to personal attacks and unwillingness to listen to others' views.

Contribute but don't dominate. If you are the kind of person who loves to talk and has a lot to say, you probably contribute more to discussions than other participants. On the other hand, if you are more reserved, you may seldom say anything. There is nothing wrong with being either kind of person. However, discussions tend to be most productive when everyone contributes ideas. For this to happen, loquacious people need to exercise a little restraint, and more reserved people need to accept responsibility for sharing their thoughts.

Avoid distracting speech mannerisms. Such mannerisms include starting one sentence and then abruptly switching to another; mumbling or slurring your words; and punctuating every phrase or clause with audible pauses ("um," "ah,") or meaningless expressions ("like," "you know," "man"). These annoying mannerisms distract people from your message. To overcome them, listen to yourself when you speak. Even better, tape your conversations with friends and family (with their permission), then play the tape back and listen to yourself. Whenever you are engaged in a discussion, aim for clarity, directness, and economy of expression.

Listen actively. When the participants don't listen to one another, discussion becomes little more than serial monologue—each person taking a turn at speaking while the rest ignore what is being said. This can happen quite unintentionally because the mind can process ideas faster than the fastest speaker can deliver them. Your mind may get tired of waiting and wander about aimlessly like a dog off its leash. In such cases, instead of listening to the speaker's words, you may think about her clothing or hairstyle or look outside the window and observe what is happening there. Even when you make a serious effort to listen, it is easy to lose focus. If the speaker's words trigger an unrelated memory, you may slip away to that earlier time and place. If the speaker says something you disagree with, you may begin framing a reply. The best way to maintain your attention is to be alert for such distractions and to resist them. Strive to enter the speaker's frame of mind, understand what is said, and connect it with what was said previously. Whenever you realize your mind is wandering, drag it back to the task.

Judge ideas responsibly. Ideas range in quality from profound to ridiculous, helpful to harmful, ennobling to degrading. It is therefore appropriate to pass judgment on them. However, fairness demands that you base your judgment on thoughtful consideration of the overall strengths and weaknesses of the ideas, not on initial impressions or feelings. Be especially careful with ideas that are unfamiliar or different from your own because those are the ones you will be most inclined to deny a fair hearing.

Resist the urge to shout or interrupt. No doubt you understand that shouting and interrupting are rude and disrespectful behaviors, but do you realize that in many cases they are also a sign of intellectual insecurity? It's true. If you really believe your ideas are sound, you will have no need to raise your voice or to silence the other person. Even if the other person resorts to such behavior, the best way to demonstrate confidence and character is by refusing to reciprocate. Make it your rule to disagree without being disagreeable.

Avoiding Plagiarism[12]

Once ideas are put into words and published, they become *intellectual property*, and the author has the same rights over them as he or she has over a material possession such as a house or a car. The only real difference is that intellectual property is purchased with mental effort rather than money. Anyone who has ever wracked his or her brain trying to solve a problem or trying to put an idea into clear and meaningful words can appreciate how difficult mental effort can be.

Plagiarism is passing off other people's ideas or words as one's own. It is doubly offensive in that it both steals and deceives. In the academic world, plagiarism is considered an ethical violation and is punished by a failing grade for a paper or a course or even by dismissal from the institution. Outside the academy, it is a crime that can be prosecuted if the person to whom the ideas and words belong wishes to bring charges. Either way, the offender suffers dishonor and disgrace, as the following examples illustrate:

- When a university in South Africa learned that professor Marks Chabel had plagiarized most of his doctoral dissertation from Kimberly Lanegran of the University of Florida, the university fired Chabel. Moreover, the university that had awarded him his Ph.D. revoked it.

- When U.S. Senator Joseph Biden was seeking the 1988 Democratic presidential nomination, it was revealed that he had plagiarized passages from speeches by British politician Neil Kinnock and by Robert Kennedy. It was also learned that, while in law school, he had plagiarized a number of pages from a legal article. The ensuing scandal led Biden to withdraw his candidacy and has continued to stain his reputation.

- The reputation of historian Stephen Ambrose was tarnished by allegations that over the years he plagiarized the work of several authors. Doris Kearns Goodwin, historian and advisor to President Lyndon Johnson, suffered a similar embarrassment when she was discovered to have plagiarized from more than one source in one of her books.

- When James A. Mackay, a Scottish historian, published a biography of Alexander Graham Bell in 1998, Robert Bruce presented evidence that the book was largely plagiarized from his 1973 biography, which had won a Pulitzer Prize. Mackay was forced to withdraw his book from the market. (Incredibly, he did not learn from the experience because he then published a biography of John Paul Jones, which was plagiarized from a 1942 book by Samuel Eliot Morison.)

- When *New York Times* reporter Jason Blair was discovered to have plagiarized stories from other reporters and fabricated quotations and details in his stories, he resigned his position in disgrace. Soon afterward, the two senior editors who had been his closest mentors also resigned, reportedly because of their irresponsible handling of Blair's reportage and the subsequent scandal.

Some cases of plagiarism are attributable to intentional dishonesty, others to carelessness. But many, perhaps most, are due to misunderstanding. The instructions "Base your paper on research rather than on your own unfounded opinions" and "Don't present other people's ideas as your own" seem contradictory and may confuse students, especially if no clarification is offered. Fortunately, there is a way to honor both instructions and, in the process, to avoid plagiarism.

Step 1: When you are researching a topic, keep your sources' ideas separate from your own. Begin by keeping a record of each source of information you consult. For an Internet source, record the Web site address, the author and title of the item, and the date you visited the site. For a book, record the author, title, place of publication, publisher, and date of publication. For a magazine or journal article, record the author, title, the name of the publication, and its date of issue. For a TV or radio broadcast, record the program title, station, and date of transmission.

Step 2: As you read each source, note the ideas you want to refer to in your writing. If the author's words are unusually clear and concise, copy them *exactly* and put quotation marks around them. Otherwise, *paraphrase*—that is, restate the author's ideas in your own words. Write down the number(s) of the page(s) on which the author's passage appears.

If the author's idea triggers a response in your mind—such as a question, a connection between this idea and something else you've read, or an experience of your own that supports or challenges what the author says—write it down and put brackets (not parentheses) around it so that you will be able to identify it as your own when you review your notes. Here is a sample research record illustrating these two steps:

> Adler, Mortimer J. *The Great Ideas: A Lexicon of Western Thought* (New York: Macmillan, 1992) Says that throughout the ages, from ancient Greece, philosophers have argued about whether various ideas are true. Says it's remarkable that most renowned thinkers have agreed about what truth is—"a correspondence between thought and reality." 867 Also says that Freud saw this as the *scientific* view of truth. Quotes Freud: "This correspondence with the real external world we call truth. It is the aim of scientific work, even when the practical value of that work does not interest us." 869 [I say true statements fit the facts; false statements do not.]

Whenever you look back on this record, even a year from now, you will be able to tell at a glance which ideas and words are the author's and which are yours. The first three sentences are, with the exception of the directly quoted part, paraphrases of the author's ideas. Next is a direct quotation. The final sentence, in brackets, is your own idea.

Step 3: When you compose your paper, work borrowed ideas and words into your own writing by judicious use of quoting and paraphrasing. In addition, give credit to the various authors. Your goal here is to eliminate all doubt about which ideas and words belong to whom. In formal presentations, this crediting is done in footnotes; in informal ones, it is done simply by mentioning the author's name.

Here is an example of how the material from Mortimer Adler might be worked into a composition. (Note the form that is used for the footnote.) The second paragraph illustrates how your own idea might be expanded:

> Mortimer J. Adler explains that throughout the ages, from the time of the ancient Greeks, philosophers have argued about whether various ideas are true. But to Adler the remarkable thing is that, even as they argued, most renowned thinkers have agreed about what truth is. They saw it as "a correspondence between thought and reality." Adler points out that Sigmund Freud believed this was also the scientific view of truth. He quotes Freud as follows: "This correspondence with the real external world we call truth. It is the aim of scientific work, even when the practical value of that work does not interest us."*

> This correspondence view of truth is consistent with the commonsense rule that a statement is true if it fits the facts and false if it does not. For example, the statement "The twin towers of New York's World Trade Center were destroyed on September 11, 2002," is false because they were destroyed the previous year. I may sincerely believe that it is true, but my believing in no way affects the truth of the matter. In much the same way, if an innocent man is convicted of a crime, neither the court's decision nor the world's acceptance of it will make him any less innocent. We may be free to think what we wish, but our thinking can't alter reality.

*Mortimer J. Adler, *The Great Ideas: A Lexicon of Western Thought* (New York: Macmillan, 1992), pp. 867, 869.

Applications

1. Think back on your previous schooling. How closely has your experience matched Arthur's? Explain.

2. Reflect on your powers of concentration. Do you find it difficult to ponder important matters? Are you able to prevent the casual, semiconscious drift of images from interrupting your thoughts? Do you have less control in some situations than in others? Explain.

3. Rate yourself on each of the eight characteristics of good critical thinkers that are listed on pp. 24–26. Which are you strongest in? Which weakest? If your behavior varies from situation to situation, try to determine what kinds of issues or circumstances bring out your best and worst mental qualities.

4. Consider how you approach problems and issues. Is there any pattern to the way you think about a problem or an issue? Does an image come to mind first? Or perhaps a word? What comes next? And what after that? If you can't answer these questions completely, do this exercise: Flip half a dozen pages ahead in this book, pick a sentence at random, read it, and note how your mind deals with it. (Such thinking about your thinking may be a little awkward at first. If it is, try the exercise two or three times.)

5. Read each of the following statements carefully. Then decide what question(s), if any, a good critical thinker would find it appropriate to ask.
   a. Television news sensationalizes its treatment of war because it gives us pictures only of injury, death, and destruction.
   b. My parents were too strict—they wouldn't let me date until I was sixteen.
   c. It's clear to me that Ralph doesn't care for me—he never speaks when we pass in the hall.
   d. From a commercial for a news network: "The news is changing every minute of the day, so you constantly need updating to keep you informed."
   e. The statement of an Alabama public elementary school teacher who had students recite the Lord's Prayer and say grace before meals: "I feel part of my job as a teacher is to instill values children need to have a good life."

A Difference of Opinion

The following passage summarizes an important difference of opinion. After reading the statement, use the library and/or the Internet and find what knowledgeable people have said about the issue. Be sure to cover the entire range of views. Then assess the strengths and weaknesses of each. If you conclude that one view is entirely correct and the others are mistaken, explain how you reached that conclusion. If, *as is more likely*, you find that one view is more insightful than the others but that they all make some valid points, construct a view of your own that *combines* the insights from all views and explain why that view is the most reasonable of all. Present your response in a composition or an oral report, as your instructor specifies.

What response should the United States make to the problem of illegal immigration? As violence on the southern U.S. border increases and illegal entry continues, many Americans are becoming impatient with the federal government's failure to solve the border problem. The state of Arizona has already taken action to apprehend illegals but has been criticized for interfering in matters under federal jurisdiction. Is Arizona's approach the most reasonable one? If not, what approach would be?

Begin your analysis by conducting a Google search using the terms "Arizona illegal immigrants" and "border security issues."

B. Is that the only factor that contributes to strict parents

CHAPTER 3

What Is Truth?

For hundreds of years, philosophers battled over whether "truth" exists. The argument usually concerned Truth with a capital *T*, a kind of complete record of whatever was, is, or will be, error-proof, beyond doubt and dispute, a final test of the rightness or wrongness of people's ideas and theories.

Those who accepted the existence of this Truth believed it was a spiritual reality, not a physical one. That is, it was not a celestial ledger or file drawer—yet it was beyond time and space. It was considered an understanding among the gods, or an idea in the mind of God, or simply the sum total of Reality. Could humans ever come to know Truth? Some said, no, never. Others said, yes but only in the afterlife. Still others said that the wisest and best of humans could catch glimpses of it and that the rest of humanity could learn about it through these special ones.

Those who rejected this notion of an awesome, all-embracing Truth argued that it was an empty notion. How could all reality be summed up that way? More important, what possible evidence could be offered in support of its existence? Many who reasoned this way dismissed the idea of Truth as wishful thinking, a kind of philosophical security blanket. A few went further and denied even the existence of truths (no capital).

Our age has inherited the whole argument. The focus, however, has changed. It seldom concerns Truth anymore. Even if Truth does exist, it's of little help to us in our world and our lives because it is beyond human understanding. Even many people of strong and rather conservative religious views no longer consider the question of Truth important to the understanding or practice of their faith.

Still, the question of truth, or even truths, remains, and the position we take toward this question does have an important bearing on how we conduct our thinking and acting. Unfortunately, there is a good deal of murkiness and confusion about the concept. The rest of this chapter will attempt to shed light on it.

It's fashionable today to believe that truth is relative and subjective. "Everyone creates his or her own truth," the saying goes, "and what is true for you may not be true for me." The meaning of this statement goes far beyond "It's a free country and I can believe what I want." The claim means that *whatever a person thinks is true because he or she thinks it is.* Not surprisingly, to challenge another person's view on an issue is considered bad form. "That's my truth you're talking about, Buster. Show a little respect."

The implications of this notion are quite staggering, yet for some reason few people acknowledge them, and fewer still are interested in testing their reasonableness. One implication is that everyone is right and no one is wrong. In fact, no one *can* be wrong. (What an argument this would make against objective tests—true/false, multiple choice, and so on: "My answers can't be wrong, professor. They're my truth!") Another is that everyone's perception and memory work flawlessly, with never a blunder, glitch, or gaffe. And another is that no one adopts other people's "truths." The idea of creating truth rules out borrowing—if truth is intensely personal, each person's truth must be unique. Let's examine all these ideas more closely.

Where Does It All Begin?

The idea of creating our own truth without outside influence or assistance may sound reasonable if we focus only on our adulthood. The moment we consider our childhood, however, the idea becomes suspect, because in childhood we were all dependent in every sense: physically, emotionally, and intellectually. What we knew and believed about everything was what others told us. We asked questions—"Why, Mommy?" "Why, Daddy?" Our parents answered them. We accepted those answers and made them the foundation of our belief system, no matter how elaborate it would become in adulthood.

Relativists could, of course, claim that we leave all those early influences behind when we reach adulthood, but that denies the most fundamental principles of psychology. Here is how one writer explained the continuing influence of childhood experience:

> We are told about the world before we see it. We imagine most things before we experience them. And those preconceptions, unless education has made us acutely aware, govern deeply the whole process of perception. They mark out certain objects as familiar or strange, emphasizing the difference, so that the slightly familiar is seen as very familiar, and the somewhat strange as sharply alien. They are aroused by small signs, which may vary from a true index to a vague analogy. Aroused, they flood fresh vision with older images, and project into the world what has been resurrected in memory.[1]

You have heard the old saying *seeing is believing*. The reverse—*believing is seeing*—is equally correct. To a greater or lesser extent, what we regard as our unique perspective bears the imprint of other people's ideas and beliefs.

Imperfect Perception

Is perception flawless? Hardly. For one thing, it is influenced by our desires, interests, and expectations: "From the outset perception is selective and tends to simplify the world around us. Memory continues and hastens the process."[2] For another, even within its limited focus, perception is often flawed. A college student who is positive that the textbook contains a certain statement answers an exam question with perfect confidence. Yet when the student gets the corrected test back and finds the question marked wrong, then hurriedly flips open the book and examines the passage again, he or she may find it says something else entirely.

Moviegoers in the 1930s and 1940s were thrilled as Tarzan uttered his famous yell and swung through the treetops to catch the villain. Tell them that Tarzan never made that yell and they'll say, "False, we heard it with our own ears." And yet it's not false. According to one of the men who first played the role of Tarzan, Buster Crabbe, that yell was dubbed into the films in the studio. It was a blend of three voices—a soprano's, a baritone's, and a hog caller's.

At least a dozen times every weekend from September to January, the imperfection of human observation is underlined by that marvel of technology, the instant replay. Is there a football fan anywhere who doesn't occasionally scream, "Bad call!" only to be proved wrong a moment later? We can be sure enough to bet a week's wages that the pass receiver's feet came down inbounds or that the running back's knee hit the ground before the ball came loose. And then the replay shows us how erroneous our initial perception was.

The vagaries of perception have long been noted by those who deal with human testimony—notably, trial lawyers, police officers, and psychologists. It is well established that a number of factors can make us see and hear inaccurately. Darkness, cloudy conditions, or distance from what we are witnessing may obscure our vision. We may be distracted at a crucial moment. If we are tired or in the grip of powerful emotions such as fear or anger, our normal perceptiveness may be significantly diminished. Also, perception may be intermingled with interpretation—the expectation that an event will unfold in a certain way may color our perception of the way the event actually unfolds. Loyalty and affection toward the people or things involved may distort our vision as well. If someone we dislike speaks in a loud voice and is animated, we may regard that person as showing off to get attention. But if a friend behaves in the same way, we may regard him or her as vivacious and extroverted.

Imperfect Memory

Even when our perception is initially flawless, our memory often distorts the data. We forget details, and when later attempting to recall what happened we resort to imagination to fill in the blanks. Though we may at first be aware that such a process of reconstruction is occurring, this awareness soon fades, and we come to believe we are remembering the original perception. As psychologist William James explained,

> The most frequent source of false memory is the accounts we give to others of our experiences. Such acts we almost always make more simple and more interesting than the truth. We quote what we should have said or done rather than what we really said or did; and in the first telling we may be fully aware of the distinction, but [before] long the fiction expels the reality from memory and [replaces it]. We think of what we wish had happened, of possible [interpretations] of acts, and soon we are unable to distinguish between things that actually happened and our own thoughts about what might have occurred. Our wishes, hopes, and sometimes fears are the controlling factor.[3]

As if this weren't enough, memory is vulnerable to contamination from outside the mind. Memory expert Elizabeth Loftus showed children a one-minute film and then asked, "Did you see a bear?" or "Did you see a boat?" They remembered seeing them, even though no bears or boats were in the film. She also showed adults a film of an auto accident and then asked them about it. By using the word "smash" instead of "hit," she was able to change the viewers' estimate of the cars' speed and to create a memory of broken glass where there was none. In another experiment, Loftus asked the parents of college students to describe some events from their sons' and daughters' childhoods. Then she talked with each student about those events but added a fake event or two. With only slight coaxing, the students "remembered" the fake events, were able to elaborate on the details, and in some cases refused to believe they were fake even when Loftus explained what she had done.[4]

Deficient Information

The quality of a belief depends to a considerable extent on the quality of the information that backs it up. Because it's a big world and reality has many faces, it's easy for us to be misinformed. How many drivers take the wrong turn because of faulty directions? How many people get on the wrong bus or train? How many car owners put too much or too little air in their tires on the advice of some service station attendant? And, if misinformation is common enough in such relatively simple matters, how much more common is it in complex matters like law and medicine and government and religion?

It's possible, of course, to devote a lifetime of study to a particular field. But not even those who make that kind of commitment can know everything about their subject. Things keep happening too fast. They occur whether we're watching or not. There's no way to turn them off when we take a coffee break or go to the bathroom. The college student who hasn't been home in three months may be able to picture the neighbor's elm tree vividly, yet it may have been cut down two months ago. The soldier may have total recall of his hometown—every sight and sound and smell—and return home to find half of Main Street sacrificed to urban renewal, the old high school hangout closed, and a new car in his best friend's driveway.

Even the Wisest Can Err

So far, we've established that people can be mistaken in what they perceive and remember and that the information they receive can be faulty or incomplete. But these matters concern individuals. What of *group* judgment—the carefully analyzed observations of the best thinkers, the wisest men and women of the time? Is that record better? Happily, it is. But it, too, leaves a lot to be desired.

All too often, what is taken as truth one day by the most respected minds is proved erroneous the next. You undoubtedly know of some examples. In the early seventeenth century, when Galileo suggested that the sun is the center of our solar system, he was charged with heresy, imprisoned, and pressured to renounce his error. The "truth" of that time, accepted by every scientist worthy of the name, was that the earth was the center of the solar system.

Here are some other examples you may not have heard about in which the "truth" turned out not to be true:

- For a long time surgeons used talc on the rubber gloves they wore while performing surgery. Then they discovered it could be poisonous. So they switched to starch, only to find that it, too, could have a toxic effect on surgical patients.[5]

- Film authorities were certain they were familiar with all the films the late Charlie Chaplin ever made. Then, in 1982, a previously unknown film was discovered in a British screen archive vault.[6]

- For hundreds of years historians believed that although the people of Pompeii had been trapped by the eruption of Mount Vesuvius in A.D. 79, the people of neighboring Herculaneum had escaped. Then the discovery of eighty bodies (and the hint of hundreds more) under the volcanic ash revealed that many from Herculaneum had also been trapped.[7]

- Your grandparents probably learned that there are eight planets in our solar system. Since Pluto was discovered in 1930, your parents and you learned there are nine. Then Joseph L. Brady of the University of California suggested there might be ten.[8] But more recently Pluto was removed from the list.

- After morphine was used by doctors for some years as a painkiller, it was found to be addictive. The search began for a nonaddictive substitute. What was found to take its place? Heroin![9]

Truth Is Discovered, Not Created

Let's review what our evaluation has revealed. First, our ideas and beliefs are unavoidably influenced by other people's, particularly in childhood. Second, perception and memory are imperfect. Third, our information can be inaccurate or incomplete. Add to this the fact, noted in Chapter 2, that some people's thinking skills are woefully meager and/or ineffectively used, and the idea that "everyone creates his or her own truth" becomes laughable. We do create something, all right, but it is not truth. It is *beliefs*, ideas that we accept as true but that could easily be false.

What, then, is the most reasonable view of truth? The truth about something is *what is so about it*—the facts in their exact arrangement and proportions. Our beliefs and assertions are true when they correspond to that reality and false when they do not.

Did time run out before the basketball player got the shot off? How does gravity work? Who stole your hubcaps? Are there time/space limits to the universe? Who started the argument between you and your neighbor last weekend? Have you been working up to your potential in this course? To look for the truth in such matters is to look for the answer that fits the facts, the *correct* answer.

Truth is apprehended by *discovery*, a process that favors the curious and the diligent. Truth does not depend on our acknowledgment of it, nor is it in any way altered by our ignorance or transformed by our wishful thinking. King Tut's tomb did not spring into existence when archaeologists dug it up; it was there waiting to be discovered. Art forgeries are not genuine when people are fooled and then fake when the deception is revealed. Cigarette smoking is not rendered harmless to our health because we would prefer it to be so.

Much of the confusion about truth arises from complex situations in which the truth is difficult to ascertain or express. Consider a question like Are there really UFOs that are piloted by extraterrestrial beings? Although the question is often hotly debated and people make assertions that purport to express the truth, there is not yet sufficient evidence to say we know the truth about UFOs. However, that doesn't mean there is no truth about them or that people who affirm their existence and people who deny it are equally correct. It means that whatever the truth is, we do not yet possess it.

Similar difficulty arises from many psychological and philosophical questions—for example: Why are some people heterosexual and others homosexual? Is the cause of criminality genetic or environmental or a combination of the two? Are humans inherently violent? Is there an after-life? What constitutes success? The answers to these questions, and to many of the issues you will encounter in the applications in this book, will often be incomplete or tentative. Yet that fact should not shake your conviction that there are truths to be discovered.

When planes crashed into the twin towers of the World Trade Center and the Pentagon on September 11, 2001, killing several thousand people, the event was officially classified as a terrorist attack. But before long, a very different theory was advanced—that individuals in the highest levels of the U.S. government had planned and executed the crashes to provide an excuse for attacking Iraq. This conspiracy theory gained a number of well-known supporters, including movie and television stars and at least one member of Congress, and was disseminated around the world. In France, for example, a book supporting the theory became a best-seller. The issue became the subject of international debate—in some quarters, people are still divided in their views. But to my knowledge, not a single individual, in this country or abroad, took the position that *both* views are correct—that is, that each side is entitled to its own truth. If anyone had, he or she would have been attacked by both camps for talking nonsense and trivializing an important issue. When it comes to significant events like 9/11, people want to know *the* truth, what really happened.

Having the right frame of mind can make your pursuit of the truth less burdensome and give it the sense of adventure that the great thinkers in history experienced. A good way to begin is to keep the following thought in mind: "I know I have limitations and can easily be mistaken. And surely I'll never find all the answers I'd like to. But I can observe a little more accurately, weigh things a little more thoroughly, and make up my mind a little more carefully. If I do so, I'll be a little closer to the truth."

That's far different from saying, "Everyone makes his or her own truth" or "It all depends on how you look at it." And it is much more reasonable.

Understanding Cause and Effect[10]

Some of the most difficult challenges in discovering truth occur in determining cause-and-effect relationships. Unfortunately, mistakes are common in such matters. One mistake is to see cause-and-effect relationships where there are none. Another is to see only the simple and obvious cause-and-effect relationships and miss the complex or subtle ones. A third is to believe that causation is relevant only to material forces and is unrelated to human affairs. To avoid such confusion, four facts must be understood:

1. One event can precede another without causing it. Some people believe that when one event precedes another, it must be the cause of the other. Most superstition is rooted in this notion. For example, breaking a mirror, crossing paths with a black cat, or walking under a ladder is believed to cause misfortune. You don't have to be superstitious to make this mistake. You may believe that your professor gave an unannounced quiz today because students were inattentive the day before yesterday, whereas he may have planned it at the beginning of the semester. Or you may believe the stock market fell because a new president took office, when other factors might have prompted the decline.

The problem with believing that preceding events necessarily cause subsequent events is that such thinking overlooks the possibility of *coincidence*. This possibility is the basis of the principle that "correlation does not prove causation." In order to establish a cause-and-effect relationship, it is necessary to rule out coincidence, or at least to make a persuasive case against it.

2. Not all causation involves force or necessity. The term *causation* is commonly associated with a physical action affecting a material reality, such as, a lightning bolt striking a house and the house catching fire and burning. Or a flowerpot being accidentally dropped out a window and then falling to the ground and breaking. Or a car speeding, failing to negotiate a curve, careening off the highway, and crashing into a tree. In such cases a scientific principle or law applies (combustion, gravity, inertia), and the effect is inevitable or at least highly predictable.

That type of causation is valid, but it would be a mistake to think of it as the *only* type. Causation also occurs in the nonmaterial realities we call human affairs—more specifically, in the processes of emotion and thought. That type of causation has little, if anything, to do with scientific principles or laws, is almost never inevitable, and is often difficult to predict. If we are to avoid oversimplification, we need to define causation in a way that covers both the scientific realm and the realm of human affairs. Here is a footnote for this: As its first definition of *cause*, the *Oxford English Dictionary* gives "that which produces an effect; that which gives rise to any action, phenomenon, or condition." The distinction between "produces" and "gives rise to" is what we are referring to here. We will therefore define causation as *the phenomenon of one thing influencing the occurrence of another*. The influence may be major or minor, direct or indirect, proximate or remote in time or space. It may also be irresistible, as in the examples of combustion, gravity, and inertia mentioned previously; or resistible, as in following parental teaching or the example of one's peers. In the latter case, and in other matters involving ideas, the influence (cause) does not *force* the effect to occur but instead *invites, encourages,* or *inspires* it. Consider these examples:

> The idea that intelligence is genetically determined led early twentieth-century educators to conclude that thinking cannot be taught, and thus to emphasize rote learning and expand vocational curriculums.
>
> The idea that people are naturally good, and therefore not personally responsible for their bad deeds, has shifted blame to parents, teachers, and society, and caused judges to treat criminals more leniently.
>
> The idea that one race or ethnic group is superior to another has led to military campaigns against neighboring countries, discriminatory laws, slavery, and genocide.
>
> The idea that "no one over thirty can be trusted," which was popular in the United States during the 1960s and 1970s, led many young people to scorn both the advice of their parents and teachers and the accumulated wisdom of the past.
>
> The idea that feelings are a reliable guide to behavior has led many people to set aside restraint and follow their impulses. This change has arguably led to an increase in incivility, road rage, and spouse abuse, among other social problems.
>
> The idea that self-esteem is prerequisite to success changed the traditional idea of self-improvement, inspired hundreds of books focused on self-acceptance, and led educators to more indulgent views of homework, grading, and discipline.

In each of these examples, one idea influenced the occurrence of an action or belief and, in that sense, *caused* it. Columnist George Will no doubt had this view of causation in mind when he encountered the claim that "no one has ever dropped dead from viewing 'Natural Born Killers,' or listening to gangster rap records." Will responded, "No one ever dropped dead reading 'Der Sturmer,' the Nazi anti-Semitic newspaper, but the culture it served caused six million Jews to drop dead."[11]

3. There is a wild card in human affairs—free will. So far we have noted that causation occurs through force or necessity in material events, but through *influence* in nonmaterial events—that is, in human affairs. Also, that in human affairs, effects are to some extent predictable but much less so than in material events. Now we need to consider why they are less predictable. The answer is because *people possess free will*—that is, the capacity to respond in ways that oppose even the strongest influences. Free will is itself a causative factor, and one that can trump all others. This explains why some people who grow up in the worst of circumstances—for example, in dysfunctional, abusive families or in crime-ridden neighborhoods in which the main sources of income are drug dealing and prostitution—resist all the negative influences and become decent, hardworking, and law-abiding. (It can also explain why some people who are more fortunate economically and socially fall short of those ideals.)

It has been rightly said that people can seldom choose the circumstances life places them in, but they can always choose their responses to those circumstances because they possess free will. In any investigation of causes and effects in human affairs, the factor of free will must be considered. However, *possessing* free will is no guarantee that we will *apply* it. In fact, one factor makes such application difficult. That factor is habit.

Habit inclines smokers to continue smoking, liars to continue lying, selfish people to go on being selfish, and countless people to unthinkingly embrace the latest fashion. When leading designers say "hemlines should be raised," hordes of women comply. When oversized beltless denim jeans are in vogue, hordes of young men waddle down the street, the tops of their pants at the middle of their hips and the crotches of their pants touching their knees. When iconic athletes shave their heads, legions of fans shave theirs. Resisting the force of habit is always possible but never easy.

The most difficult habits to break are those that accrue incrementally over time. Consider the acceptance of increasing violence and sex on TV and in films. In the 1950s, not much violence and sex were shown on-screen, and what was shown was tame. Then viewers were given glimpses of blood and gore and brief peeks at naked flesh. Year by year, the number of such scenes increased and the camera drew in a little closer and lingered a little longer over them. Over time, one thematic taboo after another was broken. Eventually violence and sexuality were joined, and themes of rape, child molestation, and even cannibalism were introduced. More recently, the industry crafted a new vehicle for assaulting the senses—the forensics program, which depicts rape-murders as they happen, then presents every gory detail of the autopsies in extreme close-up, accompanied by frequent, graphic flashbacks to refresh in viewers' minds the shocking details of the crimes.

At first the violent and sexual content provoked protests. In time, however, as sensational images became familiar, people formed the habit of accepting them, and the protests diminished. (In time the habit grew so strong that anyone who objected to graphic sex and violence was considered odd.) What happened in this case was not that people lost their freedom or ability to protest, but instead that habit took away their *inclination* to protest.

4. Causation is often complex. When a small pebble is dropped into a serene pool of water, it causes ripples in every direction, and those ripples can affect even distant waters. NASA researchers have found a similar process at work in the atmosphere: tiny particles in the air called aerosols can have a rippling effect on the climate thousands of miles away from their source region.

Effects in human affairs can also be complex. In an effort to cut costs, the owner of a chemical plant may dispose of chemicals in a nearby stream that flows into a river. This action may result in effects he did not intend, including the pollution of the river, the killing of fish, and even the contracting of cancer by people living far from his plant. Those effects will be no less real because he did not intend them.

A woman in the early stages of influenza, unaware that she is ill, may sneeze while on a crowded airplane and infect dozens of her fellow passengers. As a result, they may lose time at work; some may have to be hospitalized; those with compromised immune systems could conceivably die. Given her lack of knowledge of her condition, no reasonable person would consider her culpable (morally responsible) for the effects of her sneeze, but there would still be no doubt that she caused them.

A car is driving on the interstate at night. In rapid succession, a deer jumps out and, the driver slams on his brakes but still hits and kills the deer, the car traveling closely behind slams into his car, and five other cars do likewise, each crashing into the car in front. As a result of this chain reaction, the drivers and passengers suffer a variety of injuries— minor in the case of those wearing seat belts, major in others. The task of identifying the causative factors requires careful attention to the details. The initial cause was the deer's crossing the road at an unfortunate time, but that is not the only cause. The first driver caused the deer's demise. Each of the other drivers caused the damage to the front end of his or her car and back end of the car in front.* And the passengers who did not fasten their seat belts caused their injuries to be more severe than those of other drivers and passengers.

These examples contain a valuable lesson about the need for care in investigating causes and effects. But this lesson will be even clearer if we examine a case in the way investigation usually proceeds—*backward* in time from the latest effect to the earliest causative factor; that is, to the "root" cause.

For example, it has been clear for some time that the number of people of Middle Eastern origin living in Europe has increased so dramatically that before long, according to some observers, Europe might well be called "Eurabia." What *caused* this change? Analysts found that for decades European companies, with their governments' blessing, have

---

*At first consideration, it might seem that the front driver in each case caused the accident behind him/her. However, the law holds each driver responsible for maintaining sufficient distance to stop and avoid a crash.

been inviting foreigners to work in their countries, and these workers brought their families, formed their own enclaves, built their own mosques and churches, and "planted" their own ethnic cultures. The next question is what *caused* the governments to approve this influx of workers? The answer is that the native population of European countries had declined to a point near or below "replacement level" and there were too few native-born workers to fill the available jobs and thus fund older people's pensions and health care services.

What *caused* the population decline? The availability of effective birth control techniques in the 1960s and 1970s and the choice of more and more families to employ those techniques. What *caused* so many families to limit the number of their children? One factor was the century-long population movement from rural areas to cities, where children are an economic burden rather than an asset. Others were the growing emphasis on self-fulfillment and the corresponding tendency to regard child rearing as self-stifling.

As even this brief analysis of causes and effects suggests, facile responses to complex issues—in this case, "Middle Easterners are trying to take over Europe" or "The Crusades are here again, in reverse"—are not only unhelpful but unfair. The following cautions will help you avoid oversimplification in your analyses:

> **Remember that events seldom, if ever, "just happen."** They occur as the result of specific influences, and these influences may be major or minor, direct or indirect, proximate or remote in time or space; also irresistible (forced or necessary) or resistible (invited, encouraged, or inspired).

> **Remember that free will is a powerful causative factor in human affairs,** and it is often intertwined with other causes. In the case of the changes in European society, the movement of people from farm to city and the use of birth control were individual choices, but the greater availability of jobs in the cities (an economic reality) and birth control technology (a scientific development) were not.

> **Be aware that in a chain of events, an effect often becomes a cause.** For example, the decline in population in Europe caused the importation of foreign workers, which in turn caused a change in the ratio of native-born to foreign citizens, which may in time alter the continent's dominant values and attitudes.

> **Be aware that, in dealing with human affairs, outcomes can be unpredictable.** Therefore, in determining causes, you may have to settle for probability rather than certainty (as you would in matters that lend themselves to scientific measurement). In other words, you might conclude that something is *more likely than not* or, when the probability is very high, *substantially more likely* to be the cause. Either of these conclusions has significantly more force than mere possibility, but it falls short of certainty. The difference is roughly analogous to the difference in legal standards of judgment: in civil cases, the standard is "a preponderance of the evidence" or "clear and convincing evidence," whereas in criminal cases it is the more demanding standard of "beyond a reasonable doubt."

In searching for truth, when you encounter possible cause-and-effect relationships, keep these cautions in mind.

Applications

1. Think of a recent situation in which someone referred inappropriately to "my truth." Write two or three paragraphs, in your own words, explaining to that person what you learned in this chapter.

2. A central question in sociology is How does society evolve? Three well-known individuals gave very different answers. Auguste Comte (1798–1857) suggested that it involved three stages: religious, metaphysical, and scientific. Herbert Spencer (1820–1903) claimed that it followed Darwinian "natural selection," in which only the fittest survive. Karl Marx (1818–1883) argued that it occurred through class conflict as a result of economic exploitation. Would belief in relativism—the idea that everyone creates his or her own truth—increase or decrease someone's motivation to analyze these three viewpoints and pursue the question of society's evolution? Explain your response.

3. Read each of the following passages, decide how reasonable it is, and explain your thinking.
   a. People who believe that "everyone creates his or her own truth" should never argue with anyone about anything. If they do, they are being inconsistent.
   b. Motivation to do anything depends on the belief that it has not yet been done. Everyone who loses something precious, say a diamond ring, will search diligently and even desperately until it is found. But only a fool would continue searching for it *after* it was found. It is no different with other kinds of searches, such as the search for truth. Once we think we have it, we stop looking.

4. For years grade school students faced this question on their science tests: "True or False—The famous rings of the planet Saturn are composed of solid material." If the students marked "true," they lost credit, because the "truth" was that Saturn's rings were composed of gas or dust. Then, in 1973, radar probes revealed that all those wrong answers had been right. Saturn's rings are, in fact, composed of solid matter.[12] This confusing case seems to suggest that *the truth changed*. Did it really? Explain.

5. The scene is a campus security office, where two students are being questioned. A few minutes earlier, they were engaged in a fistfight in the cafeteria. The campus police ask them again and again how the fight started. The stories conflict. Because each student seems genuinely convinced that the other one was the aggressor and there were no witnesses, the campus police have no hope of discovering the truth. But is there a truth to discover? Or are there two truths, one for each student's story? What light does the chapter shed on these questions? *conspiracy theories could be true*

6. A strange phenomenon that affects a tiny number of the world's inhabitants has interested psychologists for some time. It occurs during what Norwegians call the "murky time," the two months each year during which areas above the Arctic Circle experience almost unrelieved darkness. The effects on people have been discovered to be unfortunate, even dangerous. At worst, people experience severe tenseness, restlessness, fear, a preoccupation with thoughts of death and even suicide. At best, they experience an inability to concentrate, fatigue, a lack of enthusiasm for anything, suspicion, and jealousy. Part of the cause is seen as lack of sleep. Accustomed to day and night, people become confused by constant darkness.[13] This phenomenon poses an interesting test of truth. Would it

be proper to say the phenomenon was true before it was recognized and acknowledged by psychologists? Or did it become true only when they became aware of it? And what of your relationship to the phenomenon? Before you became aware of it for the first time, whether reading it here or elsewhere, it was not "true to you." But did that make it any less true? Explain in light of this chapter.

7. Evaluate the following dialogues in light of what you learned in this chapter. If you lack sufficient knowledge to judge the issue, do some research.

a. *Martha:* I don't care what the courts say about abortion—I'm convinced it's murder because the fetus is a human being.
Marian: If you want to believe that, fine. Just don't impose your beliefs on others and prevent them from exercising their rights.
Martha: You don't seem to understand. It's not just a fetus in my uterus that's human but the fetus in the uterus of every pregnant woman.
Marian: Nonsense. You have no right to classify what exists in someone else's uterus. That's her business. You should mind your own business.

b. *Barbi:* Television shows about suicide should not be aired.
Ken: Why?
Barbi: Because they cause people to commit suicide.
Ken: That's ridiculous. How can a drama or documentary that shows the tragedy of suicide cause people to commit suicide?
Barbi: I don't know how it happens. Maybe some people have thoughts of suicide already and the show reinforces them. Or maybe they focus on the act of suicide and lose sight of the tragedy. All I know is that attempted suicides increase after the airing of such shows.

c. *Mabel:* I notice that when you get a newspaper you immediately turn to the astrology column. Do you really believe that nonsense?
Alphonse: It's not nonsense. The planets exercise a powerful influence on our lives; their positions in the heavens at the time of our birth can shape our destiny.
Mabel: I can't believe I'm hearing such slop from a science major.
Alphonse: What you fail to understand is that astrology is science, one of the most ancient sciences at that.

d. *Jake:* What did you think of the chapter "What Is Truth?"
Rocky: It's stupid.
Jake: What do you mean?
Rocky: It contradicts Chapter 1.
Jake: I didn't get that impression. Where's the contradiction?
Rocky: In Chapter 1 the author says that we should strive to be individuals and think for ourselves. Now he says that his idea about truth is OK and ours isn't and that we should follow his. That's a contradiction.

8. *Group discussion exercise:* How many times have you been certain something was true, only to find out later that it was not? Discuss those experiences with two or three classmates. Be prepared to share the most dramatic and interesting experiences with the rest of the class.

A Difference of Opinion

The following passage summarizes an important difference of opinion. After reading the statement, use the library and/or the Internet and find what knowledgeable people have said about the issue. Be sure to cover the entire

range of views. Then assess the strengths and weaknesses of each. If you conclude that one view is entirely correct and the others are mistaken, explain how
you reached that conclusion. If, *as is more likely,* you find that one view is
more insightful than the others but that they all make some valid points, construct a view of your own that *combines* the insights from all views and explain
why that view is the most reasonable of all. Present your response in a composition or an oral report, as your instructor specifies.

Who is responsible for the fiscal crisis of 2008? This issue continues to be
central to overcoming the consequences of the crisis and to ensuring that it
does not recur. Commentators are divided on the cause. Some claim it is was
the policies of George W. Bush's administration; others, the policies of the
Clinton administration; others, the greed of Wall Street executives. Many
point, instead, to congressional pressure on banks, during the 1990s, to give
loans to people who could not afford to repay them. Still others say the crisis
originated during the Carter administration, specifically in the Community
Reinvestment Act of 1977.

Begin your analysis by conducting a Google search using the terms "Community
Reinvestment Act," "causes financial crisis," and "subprime mortgage crisis."

CHAPTER 4

What Does It Mean to Know?

Sally looks up from her composition and asks her roommates, "How do you spell *embarrass*?"

Nancy says, "I'm not sure. I think it has a double *r* and a double *s*. Oh, I really don't know."

Marie smiles her smug smile. "I guess spelling isn't your cup of tea, Nancy. The correct spelling is e-m-b-a-r-a-s-s. Only one *r*."

By this time Sally has already opened her dictionary. "Might as well check to be sure," she says. "Let's see, *embargo, embark* . . . here it is, *embarrass*. Double *r* and double *s*. You were right, Nancy."

Let's consider what happened more closely. Marie *knew* the answer, but she was wrong. Nancy *didn't know,* but she was right. Confusing. What kind of thing can this *knowing* be? When you're doing it, you're not doing it. And when you aren't, you are.

Fortunately, it only appears to be that way. The confusion arises because the feelings that accompany knowing can be present when we don't know. Marie had those feelings. She no longer wondered or experienced any confusion; she was sure of the answer. Yet she was mistaken.

Requirements of Knowing

Nancy was in a better position than Marie because she answered correctly. Yet she didn't know, for knowing involves more than having the right answer. It also involves *the realization that you have it.*

The issue, of course, may not always be as simple as the spelling of a word. It may require understanding numerous details or complex principles or steps in a process. (It may also involve a skill—knowing *how to do* something. But that is a slightly different use of the word than concerns us here.)

Knowing usually implies something else, too—the ability to express what is known and how we came to know it. This, however, is not always so.

47

Knowing involves the realization that you have it

1 requirement of knowing — realization

We may not be able to express our knowledge in words. The best we may be able to say is "I just know, that's all" or "I know because I know." Yet these replies are feeble and hardly satisfy those who wish to verify our knowledge or acquire it.

Testing Your Own Knowledge

Following are some items of "common knowledge." Determine how many you already know, and then decide, if possible, how you came to know each. Complete this informal inventory before continuing with the chapter.

1. Women are nurturing but men are not. *False*
2. African Americans had little or no part in settling the American West. *F*
3. Expressing anger has the effect of reducing it and making us feel better.
4. The Puritans were "prim, proper, and prudish prigs."
5. Before Columbus arrived in the New World, Native Americans lived in peace with one another and in respectful harmony with the environment.
6. Alfred Kinsey's research on human sexuality is scrupulously scholarly and objective.
7. Employers import unskilled labor from other countries to save money.
8. The practice of slavery originated in colonial America.

It would be surprising if you did not think you knew most of these items. After all, many writers have written about them, and they are widely accepted as conventional wisdom. But let's look a little more closely at each of them.

1. Barbara Risman became curious about this idea and decided to study it further. Her findings challenged the conventional wisdom. Apparently, men who are responsible for caring for children or elderly parents display the same nurturing traits usually associated with women. She concluded that these traits are as dependent on one's role in life as on one's sex.[1]
2. The facts contradict what is known. For example, 25 percent of the cowboys in Texas cattle drives were African American, as were 60 percent of original settlers of Los Angeles.[2] The reason these facts are not more widely known is probably because of scholarly omission of information about African Americans from the history books.
3. Conventional wisdom again is wrong. After reviewing the evidence about anger, Carol Tavris concludes, "The psychological rationales for ventilating anger do not stand up under experimental scrutiny. The weight of the evidence indicates precisely the opposite: expressing anger makes you angrier, solidifies an angry attitude, and establishes

a hostile habit. If you keep quiet about momentary irritations and distract yourself with pleasant activity until your fury simmers down, chances are you will feel better, and feel better faster, than if you let yourself go in a shouting match."[3]

4. Although the Puritans did hold that sex is rightly reserved for marriage, they did not hesitate to talk openly about the subject and were not prudish *within* marriage. The problem seems to be that people confuse the Puritans with the Victorians.[4]

5. This is pure myth. Few tribes were completely peaceful, and many not only were warlike but slaughtered women and children and tortured their captives. Some tribes also offered human sacrifices, murdered the elderly, and practiced cannibalism. As to their alleged harmonious respect for nature, many tribes deforested the land and wantonly killed whole herds of animals.[5]

6. Alfred Kinsey's work on human sexuality has been regarded as objective, scholarly, and definitive for more than half a century. In fact, it has become a foundation of psychotherapy, education, and even religion. Amazingly, in all that time no one read it critically until Judith A. Reisman and Edward W. Eichel did so. They document that Kinsey approached his work with a firm bias that significantly influenced his conclusions. He sought to establish that exclusive heterosexuality is abnormal and results merely from conditioning and inhibition; that sex between a man and a woman is no more natural than sex between two men, two women, a man and a child, or a man and an animal; and that bisexuality should be considered the norm for human sexuality. When Abraham Maslow demonstrated to Kinsey that his approach was unscientific, Kinsey simply ignored him. Kinsey went on to assert that incest can be satisfying and enriching and that children are upset by adult sexual advances solely because of the prudishness of parents and legal authorities. The authors also allege that in his research Kinsey employed a group of nine sex offenders to manually and orally stimulate to orgasm several hundred infants and children.[6]

7. The fact is that in many cases imported labor costs more money than domestic labor when the cost of transporting the workers is included in the calculation. For example, Indian workers were chosen over local Africans to build a railroad in East Africa. Similarly, Chinese workers were chosen over colonial Malayans. In both cases, the total cost of using imported workers was greater, *but the cost per unit of work was lower because the imported workers produced more.* In these and many other cases, the principal reason for choosing foreign over domestic labor is that the foreign workers are "more diligent, reliable, skilled, or careful."[7]

8. This notion is also mistaken. Slavery is thousands of years old, predating Islam, Buddhism, and Christianity. It was practiced by the Venetians, Greeks, Jews, Chinese, Indians, and Egyptians, among others. Native American tribes enslaved one another long before the

time of Columbus. The distinction enjoyed by the Americas is not having *introduced* slavery, but having *abolished* it. Slavery was abolished in the Western Hemisphere many decades before it was in Africa, Asia, and the Middle East.[8]

The more of the eight items you "knew," and the surer you were of your "knowledge," the more troubling you are likely to find these facts. You may, in fact, be thinking, "Wait a minute, there must be some mistake. Who are these people Ruggiero is quoting? Are they genuine scholars? I'm skeptical of the whole lot of them." This reaction is understandable, because familiarity with a false statement can make it seem true. Yet it is a reaction critical thinkers keep on a short leash. The ancient Greek philosopher Epictetus's warning is relevant: "Get rid of self-conceit. For it is impossible for anyone to begin to learn that which he thinks he already knows."

Are you still troubled by our debunking of the conventional wisdom? Then consider that, for centuries, conventional wisdom also held that heavier objects fall more rapidly than lighter ones and that the heart and not the brain is the seat of consciousness.[9] It also rejected the idea that machines could ever fly, enable people to communicate with one another across town, or create pictures of the interior of the human body. That such "wisdom" is really shortsightedness is plain to us only because some individuals were willing to ask, Is it possible that what I and other people think we know isn't really so? This little question is one of the most useful tools in critical thinking.

How We Come to Know

We can achieve knowledge either actively or passively. We achieve it actively by direct experience, by testing and proving an idea (as in a scientific experiment), or by reasoning. When we do it by reasoning, we analyze a problem, consider all the facts and possible interpretations, and draw the logical conclusion.

We achieve knowledge passively by being told something by someone else. Most of the learning that takes place in the classroom and the kind that happens when we watch TV news reports or read newspapers or magazines is passive. Conditioned as we are to passive learning, it's not surprising that we depend on it in our everyday communication with friends and co-workers.

Unfortunately, passive learning has a serious defect. It makes us tend to accept uncritically what we are told even when what we are told is little more than hearsay and rumor.

Did you ever play the game Rumor (or Telephone)? It begins when one person writes down a message but doesn't show it to anyone. Then the person whispers it, word for word, to another person. That person, in

Active knowledge example — Direct experience/testing
Passive knowledge ex — Being told/teachers or TV

turn, whispers it to still another, and so on, through all the people playing the game. The last person writes down the message word for word as he or she hears it. Then the two written statements are compared. Typically, the original message has changed, often dramatically, in passing from person to person.

That's what happens in daily life. No two words have precisely the same shades of meaning. Therefore, the simple fact that people repeat a story in their own words rather than in exact quotation changes the story. Then, too, most people listen imperfectly. And many enjoy adding their own creative touch to a story, trying to improve on it by stamping it with their own personal style. This tendency may be conscious or unconscious. Yet the effect is the same in either case—those who hear it think they know.

This process is not limited to everyday exchanges among people. It is also found among scholars and authors: "A statement of opinion by one writer may be re-stated as a fact by another, who may in turn be quoted as an authority by yet another; and this process may continue indefinitely, unless it occurs to someone to question the facts on which the original writer based his opinion or to challenge the interpretation he placed upon those facts."[10]

Why Knowing Is Difficult

One reason why knowing is difficult is that some long unanswered questions continue to resist solution, questions like What causes cancer? What approach to education is best for children? and How can we prevent crime without compromising individual rights?

Another reason is that everyday situations arise for which there are no precedents. When the brain procedure known as frontal lobotomy was developed to calm raging violence in people, it raised the question of the morality of a cure that robbed the patient of human sensibilities. When the heart transplant and the artificial heart became realities, the issue of which patients should be given priority was created, as well as the question of how donors were to be obtained. When smoking was definitely determined to be a causative factor in numerous fatal diseases, we were forced to examine the wisdom of allowing cigarette commercials to mislead TV viewers and entice them into harming themselves. More recently, when smoking was shown to harm the nonsmoker as well as the smoker, a debate arose concerning the rights of smokers and nonsmokers in public places.

Still another reason why knowing is difficult is that, as one generation succeeds another, knowledge is often forgotten or unwisely rejected. For example, the ancient Greeks knew that whales have lungs instead of gills and therefore are mammals. Later, however, the Romans regarded whales as fish, a false notion that persisted in Western minds until the seventeenth century. In that century one man suggested that whales are really mammals, another later established it as fact, and the West redis-covered an item of knowledge.[11]

In our time the ideas of "sin" and "guilt" have come to be regarded as useless and even harmful holdovers from Victorian times. The "new morality" urged people to put aside such old-fashioned notions as obsta-cles to happiness and fulfillment. Then Karl Menninger, one of America's leading psychiatrists, wrote a book called *Whatever Became of Sin?* in which he argues that the notions of "sin" and "guilt" are good and necessary in civilized society.[12] He says, in other words, that our age rejected those concepts too quickly and quite unwisely. — Why?

Knowledge is often thought of as dead matter stored on dusty shelves in dull libraries. Unfortunately, the hushed atmosphere of a library can suggest a funeral chapel or a cemetery. But the appearance is deceiving. The ideas on those shelves are very much alive—and often fighting furi-ously with one another. Consider the following cases.

The idea that Columbus was the first person from Europe, Africa, or Asia to land on the shores of North or South America hangs on tena-ciously. The opposing idea challenges this again and again. (The evidence against the Columbus theory continues to mount: the discovery of ancient Japanese pottery in Ecuador, traces of visits by seafarers from Sidon in 541 B.C. as well as by the Greeks and Hebrews in A.D. 200 and by the Vikings in A.D. 874.[13] The most recent evidence suggests that the Chinese may have discovered America by 2500 B.C.)[14]

The idea that a history of slavery and deprivation has caused African Americans to have less self-esteem than whites was well established. Then it was challenged by two University of Connecticut sociologists, Jerold Heiss and Susan Owens. Their studies indicate that the self-esteem of middle-class African Americans is almost identical to that of middle-class whites and that the self-esteem of lower-class African Americans is *higher* than that of lower-class whites.[15]

The notion that when the youngest child leaves home, middle-aged parents, especially mothers, become deeply depressed and feel that life is over for them has many believers. Yet at least one study attacks that notion. It shows that many, perhaps most, parents are not depressed at all; rather, they look forward to a simpler, less demanding, life.[16]

Similarly, until recently, most scientists accepted that senility is a result of the physical deterioration of the brain and is both progressive and irreversible. Then experimenters in an Alabama veterans' hospital found that in many cases the symptoms of senility—confusion, disorien-tation, and withdrawal from reality—can be halted and even reversed by "a simple program of keeping the aged constantly in touch with the sur-rounding environment."[17]

Knowledge being tested and considering more possibilities

Books and articles referring to athletes' "second wind" abound. Yet Nyles Humphrey and Robert Ruhling of the University of Utah have presented evidence that there really is no second wind and that the sensation experienced by many athletes is merely psychological.[18]

A Cautionary Tale

Even authorities who have the most sophisticated measurement tools at their disposal fail to achieve certainty. Consider, for example, the challenge to anthropologists posed by the Tasaday tribe. When discovered on the Philippine island of Mindanao in the late 1960s, the Tasaday were living a Stone Age existence—inhabiting caves in the deep jungle, ignorant of agriculture, subsisting by hunting and gathering. Manuel Elizaldo, an associate of then dictator Ferdinand Marcos, quickly became their protector, mentor, and go-between with a fascinated world. A number of anthropologists and other experts visited the tribe and studied their artifacts, language, and social structure. Except for a few skeptics, most scholars judged them to be authentic Stone Age people. Prestigious publications like *National Geographic* wrote about the Tasaday and marveled at the fact that they were such an innocent, gentle people with no words in their language for "weapon," "war," or "hostility."

In 1986, after the Marcos regime collapsed, a Swiss journalist visited the Tasaday and found them living in houses. They reportedly admitted to him that their story was an elaborate hoax perpetrated by Elizaldo. He supposedly told them when to go to the caves and put on the Stone Age act for visiting journalists and scholars. Elizaldo has denied the charge and has had the continuing support of many scientists. Douglas Yen, an ethnobiologist and early Tasaday researcher, originally sought to link the group to neighboring farming tribes, but he now believes the Stone Age circumstances were genuine. (He cites a case in which little children were shown cultivated rice and displayed amazement.) Carol Molony, a linguist and another early Tasaday scholar, is also a believer. She argues that the tribe, children as well as adults, would have to have been superb actors to eliminate all agricultural metaphors from their speech. A local priest and former skeptic, Fr. Sean McDonagh, also believes the Tasaday to be authentic and says neighboring tribes do too.

One continuing element of dispute concerns the authenticity of Tasaday tools. Zeus Salazar, a Philippine anthropologist, maintains that the loose straps attaching stones to handles suggest a poor attempt to fake Stone Age methods. Yet archaeologist Ian Glover says such looseness has been noted in authentic Stone Age implements. The Tasaday's own statements have not simplified the puzzle. They told NBC and Philippine television that their original story was true and then told ABC and British television that it was false.

How likely is it that any outside observer *knows* the real story about the Tasaday, in all its complexity? Not very. That is why, in this and similarly difficult cases, responsible people do not claim to know what happened. Instead, they speak of what it is most *plausible* to believe happened, in light of the evidence. That is how anthropologist Thomas Headland, who exhaustively researched the Tasaday case, speaks of it. He suggests that there was probably no hoax but that there were gross exaggerations and false media reports, as well as some self-fulfilling expectations by anthropologists. It is likely, he believes, that the Tasaday were once members of the neighboring farming tribes who fled several hundred years ago (perhaps to avoid slave traders) and who hid in the forest for so many generations that they not only regressed to a Stone Age culture but lost all memory of their more advanced state.[19]

Is Faith a Form of Knowledge?

Some readers, particularly religious conservatives, may wonder whether what has been said thus far about knowledge represents a denunciation of faith. Their concern is understandable, given the number of intellectuals in this and previous centuries who have dismissed religion as mere superstition. But no such denunciation is intended here. The relationship between knowledge and religious faith is both complex and subtle. The term *religious faith* by definition suggests belief in something that cannot be proved. This is not to say that what is believed is not true, but only that *its truth cannot be demonstrated conclusively.* Jews (and many others) believe that God gave Moses the Ten Commandments, Muslims believe that Muhammad is Allah's prophet, and Christians believe that Jesus Christ is the Son of God. Science is simply not applicable to these beliefs. Philosophy can offer complementary arguments for or against them but cannot prove or disprove them.

Mortimer Adler, a distinguished philosopher, offers a very useful insight into the nature of faith:

> What is usually called a "leap of faith" is needed to carry anyone across the chasm [between philosophy and religion]. But the leap of faith is usually misunderstood as being a progress from having insufficient reasons for affirming God's existence to a state of greater certitude in that affirmation. That is not the case. The leap of faith consists in going from the conclusion of a merely philosophical theology to a religious belief in a God that has revealed himself as a loving, just and merciful Creator of the cosmos, a God to be loved, worshiped and prayed to.[20]

A related concern of religious conservatives may be whether they are compromising their faith by embracing the philosophical position expressed in this chapter. Each of us must, of course, answer this question for himself or herself. Before deciding, however, we would do well to consider the argument advanced by Mark Noll, a leading evangelical scholar. In spurning philosophical investigation, he says, evangelicals not only have removed themselves from the discussion of issues vital to all people but also have lost touch with "the habits of mind that for nearly two centuries defined the evangelical experience in America." In his view, that has proved to be a tragic mistake.[21]

Obstacles to Knowledge

Before we discuss how knowledge is best sought, let's consider two habits that *impede* knowledge: assuming and guessing. *Assuming* is taking something for granted—that is, arbitrarily accepting as true something that has not been proved or that may reasonably be disputed. Because assuming is generally an unconscious activity, we are often unaware of our assumptions and their influence on us.* The main negative effect of unrecognized assumptions is that they stifle the curiosity that leads to knowledge.

Many people, for example, never speculate about the daily life of fish. They may occasionally stop at the pet store in the mall and stare at the tank of tropical fish. But they may never display curiosity about the social roles and relationships of fish communities because they assume fish have no such roles or relationships. Yet the fact is, in the words of under-water sociologist C. Lavett Smith, "There are fish equivalents of barbers, policemen, and farmers. Some are always on the move and others are sedentary. Some work at night and some by day."[22]

Guessing is offering a judgment on a hunch or taking a chance on an answer without any confidence that it is correct. It's a common, everyday activity. For students who don't study for exams, it's a last-ditch survival technique. For an example of guessing, though, let's take a more pleasant subject—drinking beer. Some time ago a professor of behavioral science at a California college conducted a beer taste test among his students. The issue was whether they could really tell a good beer from a bad one or their favorite from others. Many students likely would guess they could, and a number of participants in the test actually guessed they could tell. However, the test showed that when the samples were not labeled, not one student could identify a single brand.[23]

Because assuming stifles curiosity and guessing denies the importance of evidence, neither is likely to lead to knowledge. The most reliable

---

*It is, of course, possible to raise assumptions to the conscious level and express them. Most scientific references to assumptions are made in this context.

approach is to be cautious in asserting that you know something. Be conservative in your level of assertion—whenever you are less than certain, speak about possibilities and probabilities. Say, "I think" or "It seems to me" rather than "I know." Most important, be honest with yourself and others about your ignorance. To admit you don't know something shows good sense, restraint, and intellectual honesty. These are not weaknesses but strengths. The admission of ignorance is the essential first step toward knowledge.

Does this mean you should be wishy-washy and hedge everything you say with maybes and perhaps? Does it mean that to be a critical thinker you must forsake convictions? The answer to both questions is an emphatic *no!* It means only that you should value firm, bold statements so much that you reserve them for occasions when the evidence permits. Similarly, you should value convictions so highly that you embrace them only when you have sufficient knowledge to do so and that you modify them whenever intellectual honesty requires.

Applications

1. Consider this statement by Greek philosopher Epictetus: "Appearances to the mind are of four kinds. Things are either what they appear to be; or they neither are nor appear to be; or they are and do not appear to be; or they are not and yet appear to be. Rightly to aim in all these cases is the wise man's task." Does this reinforce or challenge what you learned in this chapter? Explain.

2. Read the following comment by Bernard Goldberg, a journalist and author of *Bias:* "Here's one of those dirty little secrets journalists are never supposed to reveal to the regular folks out there in the audience: a reporter can find an expert to say anything the reporter wants—*anything*! Just keep on calling until one of the experts says what you need him to say and tell him you'll be right down with a camera crew to interview him. If you find an expert who says, 'You know, I think that flat tax just might work and here's why . . .' you thank him, hang up, and find another expert. It's how journalists sneak their own personal views into stories in the guise of objective news reporting."[24] What implications does this statement have for the subject of this chapter? Explain your answer.

3. In each of the following cases, someone believes he or she knows something. In light of what you learned in this chapter, discuss whether the person really does.
   a. Ted reads in the morning newspaper that a close friend of his has been arrested and charged with burglarizing a number of stores. Ted is shocked. "It's impossible. The police have made a mistake," he tells his mother. "Bob and I have been as close as brothers. I just know he's not guilty."
   b. *Ralph:* Here, Harry, try my antiperspirant. It really stops wetness.
   Harry: No, thanks. I'm suspicious of antiperspirants. It seems to me that anything designed to block a normal body function may do a lot of harm. I wouldn't be surprised if it caused cancer.

Ralph: Don't be foolish. I know it doesn't cause cancer. Products like these are carefully tested before they're allowed to be sold. If it caused cancer, it would be banned.

c. Jane: I just read there's some evidence that aspirin can prevent heart attacks. *Jenny:* That's a lot of nonsense. I know it can't. My uncle took lots of aspirin and he died of a heart attack last year.

4. "Man Is Released in Wrong Rape Charges," "Traditional Idea Debunked," "Ex-Aide Admits Lying About Lawmakers"—daily newspapers contain numerous stories like these, stories showing how what was "known" a week, a month, or years ago has been found to be false. Find at least three examples of such stories in current or recent newspapers.

5. "It ain't what a man doesn't know that makes him a fool, but what he does know that ain't so," wrote Josh Billings, a nineteenth-century American humorist. Recall as many occasions as you can in which your own experience confirmed his observation.

6. A court case pitting the U.S. government against the American Indian Movement was conducted quietly in South Dakota in late 1982. The government sought to end the Native American group's twenty-month occupation of public land in the Black Hills National Forest. The group claimed that the area was a holy land to them—their birthplace, the graveyard of their ancestors, and the center of their universe—and therefore should be turned into a permanent, religion-based Native American community. The government maintained that the group had no legal claim to the land. What factors do you think should be considered in a case like this, and what solution would best serve the interests of justice? In answering, be sure to distinguish carefully between what you know and what you assume, guess, or speculate. After answering these questions, check out the most up-to-date version of the story on the Internet. Use the search term "American Indian Movement Black Hills National Forest."

7. In recent years there has been much discussion of the insanity plea as a legal defense. Many believe it should be abolished, but many others regard it as an essential part of any reasonable criminal justice system. What is your position? In answering, be sure to distinguish carefully between what you know and what you assume or guess. If your knowledge is very limited, you might want to do some research.

8. *Group discussion exercise:* Decide if you know whether each of the following statements is accurate. Discuss your decisions with two or three classmates. Be sure to distinguish knowing from guessing or assuming.
   a. Most criminals come from lower economic backgrounds.
   b. African Americans are victims of crimes more often than are whites.
   c. The U.S. Constitution guarantees every citizen the right to own a handgun.
   d. Violence in the media is responsible for real-life violence.

A Difference of Opinion

The following passage summarizes an important difference of opinion. After reading the statement, use the library and/or the Internet and find what knowledgeable people have said about the issue. Be sure to cover the entire range of views. Then assess the strengths and weaknesses of each. If you conclude that one view is entirely correct and the others are mistaken, explain how you reached that conclusion. If, *as is more likely,* you find that one view is more insightful than the others but that they all make some valid points, construct a view of your own that *combines* the insights from all views and explain why that view is the most reasonable of all. Present your response in a composition or an oral report, as your instructor specifies.

Is the threat of global warming real or imaginary? As recently as the 1970s, many scientists were warning of the dangers, not of global warming, but of global cooling. Nevertheless, the most widely publicized alarms today concern global warming. For example, Bob Corell, Senior Fellow of the American Meteorological Society, notes that the earth's glaciers are receding at an alarming rate and that the ice field surrounding the North Pole has already shrunk dramatically. In all, approximately 105 million acres of ice have melted in the past fifteen years alone. The cause of this change, he believes, is the carbon dioxide created by human activity, notably through the burning of fossil fuels. The result, he predicts, will be a rise in sea level of 3 feet over the next 100 years and the inundation of low-lying coastal areas in every country on earth.[25]

But not all scientists agree. For example, Richard Lindzen, Professor of Atmospheric Science at Massachusetts Institute of Technology (MIT), maintains that claims of global warming are "junk science" that is being hyped by people with a "vested interest in alarm." Lindzen argues that even when the data published by such people are accurate, they do not support the conclusions drawn and the dire predictions made. Moreover, he claims that experts who dare to challenge the official view of global warming are being intimidated into silence, notably by threats that their research funding will be cut off and their publications suppressed. In support of this claim, he cites his own experience and that of scientists in several other countries.[26]

(Compounding the difficulty of this issue is the fact that in 2009 it was learned that some prominent scientists, in email exchanges, seemed to be condoning the manipulation of research data to support the global warming thesis.)

Begin your analysis by conducting a Google search using the term "controversy global warming."

PART TWO

The Pitfalls

The first seven chapters explored the context in which thinking occurs. You now know, popular notions notwithstanding, that individuality doesn't come automatically but must be earned again and again, that critical thinking is as applicable to your own ideas as it is to other people's, that truth is discovered rather than created and genuine knowledge is elusive, that opinions are only as good as the evidence that supports them, and that argument is a matter not of scoring points or shouting down others but of compiling accurate information and reasoning logically about it.

In this section we will examine the various errors that can impair thinking. We will also consider how you can best discover them in other people's writing and speaking and avoid them in your own. The most basic error, "mine-is-better" thinking, seems rooted in our human nature and paves the way for many of the other errors. The other errors are grouped according to when they occur. *Errors of perspective* are erroneous notions about reality that are present in our minds more or less continuously. *Errors of procedure* occur when we are dealing with specific issues, *errors of expression* when we put our thoughts into words, and *errors of reaction* when someone criticizes or challenges a statement or argument we have made. The final chapter in this section explores how these errors can occur in combination.

CHAPTER 6

The Basic Problem: "Mine Is Better"

> Our beliefs have been imbibed, how or why we hardly know. . . . But let a question be raised as to the soundness of our notions . . . and at once we find ourselves filled with an illicit passion for them; we defend them just as we would defend a punched shoulder. The problem, how reasonable they really are, does not trouble us. We refuse to learn truth from a foe.[1]

This observation was made by a scholar pondering the all-too-common tendency to justify beliefs rather than refine and improve them. This tendency is puzzling. People profess enthusiasm for personal growth and development and spend billions of dollars on self-help books, tapes, and seminars, yet they act as if their minds have no need of improvement.

This tendency is attributable to a "mine-is-better" perspective, which we all have to a greater or lesser extent. It is natural enough to like our own possessions better than other people's.* Our possessions are extensions of ourselves. When first-graders turn to their classmates and say, "My dad is bigger than yours" or "My shoes are newer" or "My crayons color better," they are not just speaking about their fathers or shoes or crayons. They are saying something about themselves: "Hey, look at me. I'm something special."

Several years later, those children will be saying, "My car is faster than yours" or "My football team will go all the way this year" or "My marks are higher than Olivia's." (That's one of the great blessings for students—although they may have to stoop to compare, they can usually find someone with lower grades than theirs.)

Even later, when they've learned that it sounds boastful to *say* their possessions are better, they'll continue to *think* they are: "My house is more expensive, my club more exclusive, my spouse more attractive, my

*One exception to the rule occurs when we are *envying* others. But that is a special situation that doesn't contradict the point being made here.

94

children better behaved, my accomplishments more numerous, and my ideas, beliefs, and values more insightful and profound than other people's."

All of this, as we have noted, is natural, though not especially noble or virtuous or, in many cases, even factual—simply natural. The tendency is probably as old as humanity. History records countless examples of it. Most wars, for example, can be traced to some form of "mine-is-better" thinking. Satirists have pointed their pens at it. Ambrose Bierce, for instance, in his *Devil's Dictionary*, includes the word *infidel*. Technically, the word means "one who is an unbeliever in some religion." But Bierce's definition points up the underlying attitude in those who use the word. He defines *infidel* this way: "In New York, one who does not believe in the Christian religion; in Constantinople, one who does."[2]

The results of a survey of a million high school seniors illustrate the influence of "mine-is-better" thinking. The survey addressed the question of whether people considered themselves "above average." Fully 70 percent of the respondents believed they were above average in leadership ability, and only 2 percent believed they were below average. Furthermore, 100 percent considered themselves above average in ability to get along with others, 60 percent considered themselves in the top 10 percent, and *25 percent considered themselves in the top 1 percent*.[3] (Perhaps this inflated view is partly responsible for the conviction of many students that if they receive a low grade, the teacher must be at fault.)

For many people, most of the time, the "mine-is-better" tendency is balanced by the awareness that other people feel the same way about their things, that it's an unavoidable part of being human to do so. In other words, many people realize that we all see ourselves in a special way, different from everything that is not ourselves, and that whatever we associate with ourselves becomes part of us in our minds. People who have this understanding and are reasonably secure and self-confident can control the tendency. The problem is, some people do not understand that each person has a special viewpoint. For them, "mine is better" is not an attitude that everyone has about his or her things. Rather, it is a special, higher truth about their particular situation. Psychologists classify such people as either egocentric or ethnocentric.

Egocentric People

Egocentric means centered or focused on oneself and interested only in one's own interests, needs, and views. Egocentric people tend to practice *egospeak*, a term coined by Edmond Addeo and Robert Burger in their book of the same name. Egospeak, they explain, is "the art of boosting our own egos by speaking only about what we want to talk about, and not giving a hoot in hell about what the other person wants to talk about."[4] More important for our discussion is what precedes the outward expression of self-centeredness and energizes it: egocentric people's habit of mind. Following Addeo and Burger, we might characterize that habit as *egothink.*

Because the perspective of egothink is very limited, egocentric people have difficulty seeing issues from a variety of viewpoints. The world exists for them and is defined by their beliefs and values: What disturbs them should disturb everyone; what is of no consequence to them is unimportant. This attitude makes it difficult for egocentric people to observe, listen, and understand. Why should one bother paying attention to others, including teachers and textbook authors, if they have nothing valuable to offer? What incentive is there to learn when one already knows everything worth knowing? For that matter, why bother with the laborious task of investigating controversial issues, poring over expert testimony, and evaluating evidence when one's own opinion is the final, infallible arbiter? It is difficult, indeed, for an egocentric person to become proficient in critical thinking.

Ethnocentric People

Ethnocentric means excessively centered or focused on one's group. Note the inclusion of the word "excessively." We can feel a sense of identification with our racial-ethnic group, religion, or culture without being ethnocentric. We can also prefer the company of people who share our heritage and perspective over the company of others without being intolerant. The familiar is naturally more comfortable than the unfamiliar and to pretend otherwise is to delude ourselves. Accordingly, the fact that Korean Americans tend to associate almost exclusively with one another or that the local Polish American club does not issue invitations to Italians, Finns, or African Americans should not be regarded as a sign of ethnocentrism.

What distinguishes ethnocentric individuals from those who feel a normal sense of identification with their group is that ethnocentric people believe (a) that their group is not merely different from other groups but fundamentally and completely superior to them and (b) that the motivations and intentions of other groups are suspect. These beliefs create a bias that blocks critical thinking. Ethnocentric people are eager to challenge the views of other groups but unwilling to question the views of their own group. As a result, they tend to respond to complex situations with oversimplifications. They acknowledge no middle ground to issues—things are all one way, *the way that accords with their group's perspective.* They also tend to form negative stereotypes of other groups, as psychologist Gordon Allport explained many years ago:

> By taking a negative view of great groups of mankind, we somehow make life simpler. For example, if I reject all foreigners as a category,

I don't have to bother with them—except to keep them out of my country. If I can ticket, then, all Negroes as comprising an inferior and objectionable race, I conveniently dispose of a tenth of my fellow citizens. If I can put the Catholics into another category and reject them, my life is still further simplified. I then pare again and slice off the Jew . . . and so it goes.[5]

Ethnocentric people's prejudice has an additional function. It fills their need for an out-group to blame for real and imagined problems in society. Take any problem—street crime, drug trafficking, corruption in government, political assassinations, labor strikes, pornography, rising food prices—and there is a ready-made villain to blame it on: The Jews are responsible—or the Italians, African Americans, or Hispanics. Ethnocentrics achieve instant diagnosis—it's as easy as matching column a to column b. And they get a large target at which they can point their anger and fear and inadequacy and frustration.

Controlling "Mine-Is-Better" Thinking

It's clear what the extreme "mine-is-better" attitude of egocentric and ethnocentric people does to their judgment. It twists and warps it, often beyond correction. The effect of the "mine-is-better" tendencies of the rest of us is less dramatic but no less real.

Our preference for our own thinking can prevent us from identifying flaws in our own ideas, as well as from seeing and building on other people's ideas. Similarly, our pride in our own religion can lead us to dismiss too quickly the beliefs and practices of other religions and ignore mistakes in our religious history. Our preference for our own political party can make us support inferior candidates and programs. Our allegiance to our own opinions can shut us off from other perspectives, blind us to unfamiliar truths, and enslave us to yesterday's conclusions.

Furthermore, our readiness to accept uncritically those who appeal to our preconceived notions leaves us vulnerable to those who would manipulate us for their own purposes. Historians tell us that is precisely why Hitler succeeded in winning control of Germany and wreaking havoc on a good part of the world.

"Mine-is-better" thinking is the most basic problem for critical thinkers because, left unchecked, it can distort perception and corrupt judgment. The more mired we are in subjectivity, the less effective will be our critical thinking. Though perfect objectivity may be unattainable, by controlling our "mine-is-better" tendencies, we can achieve a significant degree of objectivity.

Does anything said so far in this chapter suggest that "mine is better" can *never* be an objective, accurate assessment of a situation? Decidedly not. To think that would be to fall into the fallacy of relativism (this fallacy is discussed in Chapter 9). In the great majority of cases in which two or more ideas (beliefs, theories, conclusions) are in competition, one will be more reasonable, more in keeping with the evidence, than all the others. And if you are diligent in your effort to be a critical thinker, your idea will often prove to be the best one. But that determination is properly made *after* all the ideas have been evaluated. The problem with "mine-is-better" thinking is that it tempts us to forgo evaluation and take it for granted that our idea is best.

One way to gain control of "mine-is-better" thinking is to keep in mind that, like other people, we too are prone to it and that its influence will be strongest when the subject is one we really care about. As G. K. Chesterton observed,

> We are all exact and scientific on the subjects we do not care about. We all immediately detect exaggeration in . . . a patriotic speech from Paraguay. We all require sobriety on the subject of the sea serpent. But the moment we begin to believe in a thing ourselves, that moment we begin easily to overstate it; and the moment our souls become serious, our words become a little wild.[6]

Another way to control "mine-is-better" thinking is to be alert for signals of its presence. Those signals can be found both in our feelings and in our thoughts:

- *In feelings:* Very pleasant, favorable sensations; the desire to embrace a statement or argument immediately, without appraising it further. Or very unpleasant, negative sensations; the desire to attack and denounce a statement or argument without delay.
- *In thoughts:* Ideas such as "I'm glad that experts are taking such a position—I've thought it all along" and "No use wasting time analyzing this evidence—it must be conclusive." Or ideas such as "This view is outrageous because it challenges what I have always thought—I refuse to consider it."

Whenever you find yourself reacting in any of these ways, you can be reasonably sure you are being victimized by "mine-is-better" thinking. The appropriate response is to resist the reaction and force yourself to consider the matter fair-mindedly. Chances are this won't be easy to accomplish—your ego will offer a dozen reasons for indulging your "mine-is-better" impulse—but your progress as a critical thinker depends on your succeeding. The other errors in thinking, covered in the next four chapters, are all at least aggravated by "mine-is-better" thinking.

Applications

1. Suppose you have determined that a person making a particular argument is egocentric or ethnocentric. Would that determination be sufficient cause for you to dismiss the argument? Why or why not?

2. Some people claim that contemporary American culture tends to increase rather than diminish egocentrism and ethnocentrism. If this is true, then the ability to think critically is being undermined. Study the media for evidence that supports or refutes this charge, and write a report on your findings. (Be sure to look for subtle, as well as obvious, clues—for example, the advice offered on talk shows and the appeals used in advertisements, as well as the formal statements of agencies promoting policy changes in government and elsewhere.)

3. Recall an occasion when you observed someone demonstrating one or more of the characteristics of ethnocentrism in his or her behavior. Describe the occasion, the way in which the characteristics were revealed, and the effect they had on the person's judgment.

4. Compose a summary of this chapter for the person whose ethnocentrism you described in application 3. Make it as persuasive as you can for that person. That is, focus on the particular occasion of his or her "mine-is-better" thinking and the effects of that thinking on his or her judgment.

5. Think of two illustrations of your own "mine-is-better" thinking. Describe that thinking and the way in which you first became aware of it. If you can, determine what caused you to develop that way of thinking.

6. Evaluate the following arguments as you did the arguments in Chapter 7, application 4. First identify the argument's component parts (including hidden premises) and ask relevant questions. Then check the accuracy of each premise, stated or hidden, and decide whether the conclusion is the most reasonable one. Note that checking the accuracy of the premises may require obtaining sufficient evidence to permit a judgment. (Be alert to your own "mine-is-better" thinking. Don't allow it to influence your analysis.) If you find a premise to be inaccurate or a conclusion to be less than completely reasonable, revise the argument accordingly.

   a. *Background note: Many schools around the country are experiencing significant budget reductions. Forced to cut activities from their programs, they must decide where their priorities lie. Some follow the reasoning expressed in this argument.*
   Argument: Interscholastic sports programs build character and prepare young athletes to meet the challenges of life. In addition, competition with other schools provides the student body with entertainment and an opportunity to express school spirit and loyalty. Therefore, in all budget considerations, interscholastic sports programs should be given as high a priority as academic programs.

   b. *Background note: Concerned with the rise in teenage pregnancy, the Baltimore, Maryland, school system became the first in the nation to offer Norplant, a surgically implanted contraceptive, to teenagers. School officials' reasoning was probably, at least in part, as follows:*
   Argument: Teenage pregnancy continues to rise despite efforts to educate students about the use of condoms. Norplant will effectively prevent pregnancy. Therefore, the school system should make Norplant available.

7. State and support your position on each of the following issues. Be sure to recognize and overcome your "mine-is-better" tendencies and base your response on critical thinking.

   a. Carl F. Henry, a leading evangelical theologian, warns that the widespread attitude that there are no moral standards other than what the majority approves is a threat to our country. The survival of democratic society, he suggests, depends on recognizing definite moral standards, such as the biblical criteria of morality and justice.[7]

b. A Hasidic rabbi serving a three-year term (for bank fraud) in a federal prison petitioned a U.S. district court to order the prison to provide a kosher kitchen, utensils, and diet for him. He argued that his health was failing because the food served at the prison did not meet his kosher requirements. He could eat only lettuce, oranges, apples, carrots, and dry rice cereal.[8]

c. Both heavy metal and gangsta rap music have drawn pointed criticism from a number of social critics. They argue that such music at least aggravates (and perhaps causes) antisocial attitudes and thus can be blamed for the increase in violent crime.

d. Some people believe the penalty for driving while intoxicated should be stiffened. One provision they are urging be added to the law is mandatory jail sentences for repeat offenders.

8. Read the following dialogues carefully. Note any evidence of "mine-is-better" thinking. Then decide which view in each dialogue is more reasonable and why. (Be sure to guard against your own "mine-is-better" thinking.)

a. *Background note: On a trip to Spain in November 1982, Pope John Paul II acknowledged that the Spanish Inquisition—which began in 1480 and lasted for more than 300 years and resulted in many people's being imprisoned, tortured, and burned at the stake—was a mistake.[9]*

Ralph: It's about time the Catholic church officially condemned the Inquisition.

Bernice: The pope shouldn't have admitted that publicly.

Ralph: Why? Do you think five hundred years after the fact is too soon? Should he have waited for one thousand years to pass?

Bernice: Don't be sarcastic. I mean that his statement will undoubtedly weaken the faith of many Catholics. If you love someone or something— in this case, the Church—you should do nothing to cause it shame or embarrassment. Of course the Inquisition was wrong, but it serves no good purpose to say so now and remind people of the Church's error.

b. *Background note: When an unmarried high school biology teacher in a Long Island, New York, school became pregnant, a group of parents petitioned the school board to fire her. They reasoned that her pregnancy was proof of immorality and that allowing her to remain a teacher would set a poor example for students. The school board refused to fire her.[10]*

Arthur: Good for the school board. Their action must have taken courage. Pious hypocrites can generate a lot of pressure.

Guinevere: Why do you call them hypocrites? They had a right to express their view.

Arthur: Do you mean you agree with that nonsense about the pregnant teacher being immoral and a poor example to students?

Guinevere: Yes, I suppose I do. Not that I think everybody deserves firing from his or her job in such circumstances. I think teachers are in a special category. More should be expected of them. They should have to measure up to a higher standard of conduct than people in other occupations because they are in charge of young people's education, and young people are impressionable.

9. *Group discussion exercise:* Reflect on the following statement. Does it make sense? Does anything you read in this chapter help explain it? If so, what? Discuss your ideas with two or three classmates.

It doesn't matter if everyone in the world thinks you're wrong. If you think you're right, that's all that counts.

A Difference of Opinion

The following passage summarizes an important difference of opinion. After reading the statement, use the library and/or the Internet and find what knowledgeable people have said about the issue. Be sure to cover the entire range of views. Then assess the strengths and weaknesses of each. If you conclude that one view is entirely correct and the others are mistaken, explain how you reached that conclusion. If, *as is more likely*, you find that one view is more insightful than the others but that they all make some valid points, construct a view of your own that *combines* the insights from all views and explain why that view is the most reasonable of all. Present your response in a composition or an oral report, as your instructor specifies.

Is a national identity card a good idea for America? One of the consequences of the events of 9/11/01 is heightened concern for national security. Among the proposals that have been advanced is the creation of a national identity card system. Proponents of the idea say that it would help thwart the efforts of those who would harm us and undermine our way of life. Opponents claim it would, instead, take away precious freedoms and enable the government to intrude in our lives.

Begin your analysis by conducting a Google search using the term "pro con national identity card."

CHAPTER 7

Resistance to Change

One day a woman was about to cook a roast. Before putting it in the pot she cut off a small slice. When asked why she did this, she paused, became a little embarrassed, and said she did it because her mother had always done the same thing when she cooked a roast. Her own curiosity aroused, she telephoned her mother to ask why she always cut off a little slice before cooking her roast. The mother's answer was the same: "Because that's the way my mother did it." Finally, in need of a more helpful answer, she asked her grandmother why she always cut off a little slice before cooking a roast. Without hesitating, her grandmother replied, "Because that's the only way it would fit in my pot."[1]

This story is told by Harvard professor Ellen J. Langer. She classifies it as three generations of "mindlessness." That designation is not inappropriate, though a kinder classification would be the tendency to continue doing things as we have always done them, or resistance to change. This tendency is probably as old as humankind, so examples abound—earlier in this century, "If people were meant to fly, they'd have wings" and "Women voting? Nonsense—voting is men's business"; and in our time, "I've never worn a seat belt in my life, so I'm not going to start now." Even slight changes upset our routine, threaten our established habits, challenge the familiar. They demand that we reconsider old responses, and that's unpleasant. After all, we might find that they were ill-conceived (or even mindless).

Just as we prefer patterns of behavior that we know, so we prefer ideas that are not strange or foreign sounding, ideas we're comfortable with. When Galileo said, "The earth moves around the sun," people were upset, partly because thousands of sunrises and sunsets had told them the *sun* did the moving, but also partly because they simply had never before heard of the earth's moving. The new idea threatened their fixed belief that the earth was the center of the solar system. They had that idea neatly packaged in their minds. It was a basic part of their understanding of the universe; it was intertwined with their religion. And now this upstart Galileo was demanding no less than that they untie the package, or reopen the issue.

Shortly after the advent of bicycles, one person said it would undermine "feminine modesty." And physicians said it would cause "nymphomania," "hysteria," "voluptuous sensations," "lubricious overexcitement," and "sensual madness."[2] Some people considered the movement to restrict child labor in sweatshops a communist plot. And when astronauts first landed on the moon, at least one elderly man expressed total disbelief. "It's a trick thought up by the TV people," he said. "It's impossible for a man to reach the moon."

Insecurity and Fear

Why do we resist change? Mainly because the new and unfamiliar challenge our "mine-is-better" thinking and threaten our sense of security. In many of us that sense is very fragile. Insecurity is the reason some people will go to elaborate lengths to explain away new ideas they cannot cope with. For example, the child whose father is in jail and whose mother steals to support him may believe "all cops are bad." Once that idea becomes fixed, he may cling to it. As a result, even years later he may reject the police officer who offers him genuine concern and friendship.

Another reason people resist change is that they're afraid of the unknown. In some ways this fear may be caused by insecurity; in others it may itself cause insecurity. "Who knows what will happen if . . . ?" they wonder, and they are inclined to suspect the worst. Fired by that suspicion, they fight the new idea. This kind of fearful reaction is everywhere in evidence—in education and government, in religion, in law, science, and medicine.

As late as 1948, California law prohibited the marriage of an Oriental man and a Caucasian woman. Many people are still mumbling vague warnings about the unspeakable dangers that the racial integration of schools is going to bring. And a sizable number of Americans react to the gay liberation movement somewhat like this: "If we allow them to parade their perversion in public, our young people will be corrupted and our value system destroyed."

We might be inclined to think that the problem is peculiar to the United States, but examples of fear-inspired behavior fill the history books. After all, what drove the early settlers of North America from their European homelands was one form or another of intolerance for different ideas and beliefs. Torturing and killing heretics and witches was an established practice at innumerable times and places.

Fear and Tradition

It is probably because of the interaction between insecurity and fear that people hold tradition in such high regard. Many traditions, of course, are worthwhile. They help preserve the valuable lessons of the past; they assist us in defining our loyalties and, indeed, our own identities. However, respect for tradition sometimes can be shortsighted and unwise. This is the case whenever clinging to tradition represents not careful judgment that something deserves preservation, but rather some internal panic. "Anything is worth clinging to, as long as we cling" is not a reasonable attitude.

Surely some such panic was partly responsible for the centuries-long prohibition of dissection of the dead. Despite the entreaties of medical people, who wished only to learn the secrets of the human body in order to fight disease, religious and secular authorities refused to allow autopsies. Why? Because being unheard of, the practice was considered outrageous, sacrilegious.

The task of guarding the established ways of viewing things has always been regarded by many as a sacred task. This is true even in primitive cultures. For example, the Trobriand Islanders considered sexual success a praiseworthy accomplishment. The man who was unusually successful with women was much admired and honored. Yet it was assumed that such success would be achieved only by the favored social class. If a common islander became too successful, he was resented. As one observer, Robert K. Merton, suggested, this reaction was not due to any conspiracy on the part of the Trobriand chiefs: "It is merely that the chiefs had been indoctrinated with an appreciation of the proper order of things, and saw it as their heavy burden to enforce the mediocrity of others."[3]

Of course, it isn't always fear that makes us cling to established patterns. The man in Robert Frost's poem "Mending Wall" kept repairing the wall between his land and his neighbor's not because there was still any good purpose in doing so, but only because his father had done so before him. And consider this case of uncritical dependence on past ways. A girl was told by her mother, "Never put a hat on a table or a coat on a bed." She accepted the direction and followed it faithfully for years. One day, many years later, she repeated the direction to her own teenage daughter, and the daughter asked, "Why?" The woman realized that she had never been curious enough to ask her own mother. Her curiosity at long last aroused, she asked her mother (by then in her eighties). The mother replied, "Because when I was a little girl some neighbor children were infested with lice, and my mother explained I should never put a hat on a table or a coat on a bed." The woman had spent her entire adult life following a rule she had been taught without once wondering about its purpose or validity.[4]

At times, a tradition may seem relatively unimportant and yet in a subtle way hold tremendous significance for people. In the late 1960s, for instance, the tendency of many young people to think and act and dress differently from their parents drew surprisingly angry responses from many adults. To them it represented much more than an assertion of young people's independence. In some vague way it threatened the idea of order itself, for the parent–child relationship represented only one aspect of a whole network of higher–lower relationships: God–human, leader–follower, master–servant, employer–employee, rich–poor, teacher–student. To challenge one was to challenge all. And to challenge all was to attack the very fabric of civilized society. Given this perspective, the rabid rejection of hippies and communes and peace signs was understandable. To the traditionalist, long hair and bare feet were not just matters of appearance; they were symbols of anarchy.

Despite such resistance to change, however, many new ideas do manage to take hold. We might think that when they do, those who fought so hard for them would remember the resistance they had to overcome. Ironically, however, they often forget very quickly. In fact, they sometimes display the same fear and insecurity they so deplored in others. An example occurred in psychiatry. Sigmund Freud and his followers were ostracized and bitterly attacked for suggesting that sexuality was an important factor in the development of personality. The hostility toward Freud was so strong, in fact, that his masterwork, *The Interpretation of Dreams,* was ignored when it was first published in 1900. It took eight years to sell six hundred copies of the book.[5]

Yet when Freud's ideas became accepted, he and his followers showed no greater tolerance—they ostracized and attacked those who challenged any part of his theory. Karen Horney, for example, challenged Freud's view of woman as being driven by "penis envy." She believed, too, that neurosis is caused not only by frustrated sexual drives but also by various cultural conflicts and that people's behavior is not determined by instinctual drives but can in many instances be self-directed and modified. For these theories (today widely accepted), she was rewarded with rebuke and ostracism by the Freudian dogmatists.[6]

Overcoming Resistance to Change

Is change always good? Certainly not. "For every quack who later proves to be a genius," Martin Gardner observed, "there are ten thousand quacks who prove later only to be quacks." He cited the example of Dr.

Elisha Perkins (1740–1799), "America's first great quack." Perkins' theory was that metals could draw illness out of the body, so he designed and patented a "metallic tractor," two rods of different metals, which he pulled downward over the afflicted area.[7] In this, as in many other cases, the apparent great leap forward in knowledge or technique turned out to be a giant step backward. Living in an age of unprecedented technological change, we are sometimes too quick to embrace new ideas merely because they are new and different or because we are bored with the old ones. We then suffer, at best, inconvenience and, at worst, harm to people and institutions. A case could be made that this tendency to embrace change uncritically will eventually displace the tendency to resist change uncritically. Nevertheless, the latter tendency is sufficiently rooted in human behavior that it remains dominant.

It is important to overcome resistance to change for two reasons. First, all creative ideas are by definition new and unexpected departures from the usual and the accepted. Resisting change therefore means opposing creativity and the progress it brings about. Second, resistance to change blocks the impartial judgment essential for critical thinking. Here are three tips for overcoming your resistance to change:

1. Expect yourself to react negatively to new ideas. In addition, expect your reaction to be especially strong when the new idea challenges a belief or approach you have become attached to.

2. Refuse to let your initial negative (or, for that matter, positive) reaction be the measure of the new idea. Force yourself to set aside that reaction long enough to appraise the idea fairly.

3. Judge the idea on the basis of your critical appraisal, not your initial reaction. If there are good and sufficient reasons for rejecting part or all of the idea, by all means do so. However, be honest with yourself. If your "reasons" are only excuses in disguise, acknowledge (at least to yourself) that you are too prejudiced to judge the idea fairly.

Applications

1. Evaluate the following arguments as you did the arguments in Chapter 2, application 7. First identify the argument's component parts (including hidden premises) and ask relevant questions, as shown in that chapter. Then check the accuracy of each premise, stated or hidden, and decide whether the conclusion is the most reasonable one. Note that checking the accuracy of the premises may require obtaining sufficient evidence to permit a judgment. (Be sure that you make your judgment on the evidence and not on the basis of the argument's familiarity or unfamiliarity.) If you find a premise to be inaccurate or a conclusion to be less than completely reasonable, revise the argument accordingly.

a. *Background note: One reason the court system is clogged with cases is that prisoners are filing what some regard as frivolous lawsuits against the state or federal government—for example, suits claiming their rights are being violated because the prison food doesn't meet their dietary preferences. Law books are available in the prison library for prisoners to use in preparing their lawsuits.*

Argument: Frivolous lawsuits clog the court system. The availability of law books in prison libraries encourages prisoners to file such suits. Therefore, law books should be removed from prison libraries.

b. *Argument:* The duties of the president of the United States are too numerous and complex for one individual to fulfill, so the office of the presidency should be changed from a one-person office to a three-member board.

2. Describe a tradition in your family, religion, or ethnic group that continues to be significant for you. Then describe a tradition that has lost its meaning for you. What could have contributed to that loss other than conscious evaluation and choice?

3. Think about the extent to which you tend to resist change. The following ideas will give you an opportunity to reach a tentative conclusion. Read each one, react to it, and observe your reaction. If you notice yourself resisting it at all, examine the reaction more closely and determine what parts of the chapter shed light on your resistance.

a. The national sovereignty of all countries, including the United States, should be surrendered to the United Nations, so that there will no longer be artificial boundaries separating people.

b. Cockfighting, dogfighting, and bullfighting should be televised for the enjoyment of the minority who enjoy these "sports."

c. A federal law should be passed requiring women to retain their maiden names when they marry (that is, forbidding them from adopting their husband's name).

d. Cemeteries should open their gates to leisure-time activities for the living. Appropriate activities would include cycling, jogging, fishing, nature hiking, and (space permitting) team sports.

e. Federal and state penitentiaries should allow inmates to leave prison during daytime hours to hold jobs or attend college classes. (The only ones denied this privilege should be psychopaths.)

f. Colleges should not admit any student who has been out of high school for less than three years.

g. To encourage a better turnout at the polls for elections, lotteries should be held. (Voters would send in a ballot stub as proof that they voted. Prizes would be donated by companies.)[8]

h. Retired people should be used as teachers' aides even if they lack college degrees.[9]

i. Everyone should be issued and required to carry a national identity card, identifying themselves as a U.S. citizen.[10]

j. Churches and synagogues should remove all restrictions on women's participation in liturgical and counseling services, thus permitting women to serve as priests, ministers, and rabbis.

k. Colleges should charge juniors and seniors higher tuition than that charged to freshmen and sophomores.

4. Test the reactions of three other people to one or more of the ideas in the previous application. Be selective, choosing people you believe may be shocked by the ideas. Observe their reactions. Have them explain their positions. Decide to what extent, if any, they seem to be resistant to change. (Keep in mind that it is possible for people to disagree with the idea not because they resist a change, but because they see real weaknesses in it.)

5. Read the following dialogue carefully. Note any instances of resistance to change. Decide which view is more reasonable. (Be sure you avoid resisting change yourself and judge the issue fair-mindedly.)

Background note: In past decades college officials debated whether to censor student newspapers that published stories containing four-letter words and explicit sexual references. The debate continues, but the issue has changed. Some student papers are publishing articles that make fun of African Americans, women, and homosexuals. And others are urging students to paint graffiti on campus buildings and take up shoplifting to combat conformity.[11]

Ernest: Such articles may be childish and tasteless, but that's no reason to censor them.

Georgina: Are you kidding? Minorities pay good money to go to college. And on most campuses, I'm sure, their student activity fee pays for the student newspaper. Where's the fairness in charging them for articles that insult them or that encourage lawbreaking, which ultimately costs them as taxpayers?

Ernest: Why is everything a money issue with you? So a buck or so from every student's activity fee goes to the newspaper. Big deal. That doesn't give every student the right to play fascist and set editorial policy. The articles are written in a spirit of fun or for shock value. Censorship is not the answer. If a pesky fly buzzes around your head, you don't fire an elephant gun at it. Well, maybe you do, but no sensible person does.

6. Bill Beausay, a sports psychologist, suggests that sports be rated much as films once were: X, R, or G, depending on the amount of danger and/or violence in them. He urges that children not be allowed to take part in any X-rated sport at an early age. Such sports include motorcycle and auto racing, hockey, football, boxing, and horse racing.[12] Decide whether his suggestion has merit. Be sure to avoid resistance to change.

7. Decide whether you accept or reject the following arguments. Be careful to avoid both "mine-is-better" thinking and resistance to change, and judge the issues impartially. You may wish to research the issues further before judging.

a. Beer and wine commercials should be banned from television because they glamorize drinking, leading people to associate it with love and friendship and happiness. Such associations are every bit as misleading as those used to sell cigarettes. Alcohol commercials surely are a contributing factor in the current increase in alcohol abuse by adults and children.

b. Beauty pageants today give somewhat more attention to talent than pageants did in the past. But the underlying message is the same—"Beauty in a woman is strictly a surface matter. Only those with ample bosoms, pretty faces, and trim figures need apply." These pageants make a mockery of the truth that inner beauty, character, is the real measure of a woman (or of a man).

8. *Group discussion exercise:* Discuss with two or three classmates one of the issues you examined in application 7. Be careful that your views are not affected by resistance to change. Be prepared to present your group's view(s) to the class.

CHAPTER 8

Conformity

Conformity is behaving the way others around us do. In many ways conformity is desirable. Children are conforming when they stay away from the hot stove and look both ways before crossing the street. Automobile drivers are conforming when they obey traffic signs and signals. Hospital workers are conforming when they sterilize the operating room. These cases of conformity make living safer. Conformity can also make daily activities more productive. When the employees of a department store arrive at their workplaces at the specified time each day, the store can open promptly without inconveniencing its customers. When supermarket stock clerks stock the various items in their designated places, customers can shop more efficiently.

Similarly, in a hundred different ways, from using the "up" escalator to go up, to not parking by a fire hydrant, to using the door on the right to enter or exit a building, conformity makes life less confusing for us. And by conforming to the rules of etiquette, we make it more pleasant.

Without a measure of conformity people would never learn to hold a pencil, let alone write. More complex skills, like flying a plane or operating a computer, would be impossible to acquire. How much nonconformity, after all, does the job of driving a car permit? Can we drive facing sideways or to the rear? Can we accelerate with our left hand and blow the horn with our right foot? Certainly not without some frustration. Yet these limitations are hardly cause for complaint. The safety and comfort such conformity brings us far outweigh the crimp in our creativity.

Unfortunately, conformity does not always work to our advantage. Sometimes, going along with others does not so much increase our safety or serve our convenience as it reinforces our dependency on others. Some situations require careful evaluation and judgment. In such situations, to conform with the views or actions of others out of conviction, after we have thought and decided, is reasonable. However, to conform *instead* of thinking and deciding is irresponsible.

Internal and External Pressures to Conform

As humans, we are social creatures. We must live with others and relate to them. From our earliest moments of consciousness, we learn the importance of getting along with others. Few things are more painful to most children than separation from the group. Parents sending us to our room, teachers keeping us in while friends went out to play—these were hard punishments to bear. Even more difficult was rejection by the group itself.

As we grow older, the desire to be included does not go away. It merely takes different forms. We still yearn for the recognition, acceptance, and approval of others. That yearning is intensified by the bombardment of thousands of advertisements and TV commercials: "Join the crowd—buy this." "Don't be left out—everyone who is someone has one." Young teenagers trying to be sophisticated and middle-aged people trying to be "relevant" have in common the urge to fit some prefabricated image. Conformity promises them *belonging*.

In addition to the urge to conform that we generate ourselves, there is the external pressure of the various formal and informal groups we belong to, the pressure to endorse their ideas and attitudes and to imitate their actions. Thus, our urge to conform receives continuing, even daily, reinforcement. To be sure, the intensity of the reinforcement, like the strength of the urge and the ability and inclination to withstand it, differs widely among individuals. Yet some pressure is present for everyone. And in one way or another, to some extent, everyone yields to it.

It is possible that a new member of a temperance group might object to the group's rigid insistence that all drinking of alcoholic beverages is wrong. He might even speak out, reminding the group that occasional, moderate drinking is not harmful, that even the Bible speaks approvingly of it. But the group may quickly let him know that such ideas are unwelcome in their presence. Every time he forgets this, he will be made to feel uncomfortable. In time, if he values the group's fellowship, he will refrain from expressing that point of view. He may even refrain from *thinking* it.

This kind of pressure, whether spoken or unspoken, can be generated by any group—Friday night poker clubs, churches, political parties, committees, fraternities, unions—regardless of how liberal or conservative, formal or casual it may be. The teenage gang that steals automobile accessories may seem to have no taboos. But let one uneasy member remark that he is beginning to feel guilty about his crimes and the wrath of the rest of the gang will descend on him.

Similarly, in high school and college, the crowd a student travels with has certain (usually unstated) expectations for its members. If members drink or smoke, they will often make the member who does not do so feel that she doesn't fully belong. If a member does not share their views on sex, drugs, studying, cheating, or any other subject of importance to the group, the other members will communicate their displeasure. The *way* they communicate, of course, may be more or less direct. They may tell her she'd better conform "or else." They may launch a teasing campaign against her. Or they may be even more subtle and leave her out of their activities for a few days until she asks what is wrong or decides for herself and resolves to behave more like them.

Ironically, even groups pledged to fight conformity can generate strong pressure to conform. As many young people in the 1960s learned to their dismay, many "hippie" communes were as intolerant of dissenting ideas, values, and styles of dress and living as the "straight" society they rebelled against.

The urge to conform on occasion clashes with the tendency to resist change. If the group we are in advocates an idea or action that is new and strange to us, we can be torn between seeking the group's acceptance and maintaining the security of familiar ideas and behavior. In such cases, the way we turn will depend on which tendency is stronger in us or which value we are more committed to. More often, however, the two tendencies do not conflict but reinforce each other, for we tend to associate with those whose attitudes and actions are similar to our own.

"Groupthink"

In a well-known experiment, eight students entered a laboratory. Seven were in league with the professor; the eighth was the unknowing subject of the experiment. The group was shown four lines on an otherwise blank page. The students were asked to decide which of the three lower lines (identified as A, B, and C) matched the top line in length. Line A was exactly the same length as the top line, ten inches. The other lines were much shorter or longer. Each of the seven collaborators, in turn, gave the *wrong* answer, and the pressure mounted on the unknowing subject. When he or she was asked, the choice was clear—give the obviously *right* answer and stand alone or the *wrong answer and enjoy the support of the group.* How many subjects stuck to the testimony of their own eyes? Only one out of every five who participated in the experiment.[1]

As this experiment suggests, the urge to conform can cripple thought. Yale psychologist Irving L. Janis intensively analyzed several important actions by U.S. government leaders, actions that later were shown to be unwise. The actions were Franklin Roosevelt's failure to be ready for the Japanese attack on Pearl Harbor, Harry Truman's decision to invade North Korea, John Kennedy's plan to invade Cuba, and Lyndon Johnson's decision to escalate the Vietnam War. In each case Janis found that the advisors who endorsed the decision exhibited a strong desire to concur in the group decision. Janis named this conformist tendency "groupthink."[2]

More specifically, Janis identified a number of major defects in decision making that could be attributed to this conformity. The groups he analyzed did not survey the range of choices, but rather focused on a few. When they discovered that their initial decision had certain drawbacks, they failed to reconsider. They almost never tested their own thinking for weaknesses. They never tried to obtain the judgments of experts. They expressed interest only in those views that reinforced the positions they preferred, and they spent little time considering the obstacles that would hinder the success of their plans. In each of the cases Janis studied, these defects in thinking led to untold human suffering.

In other areas the harm caused by the urge to conform is perhaps less dramatic but no less real. A single example will suggest the extent of that harm. For two or three decades, many educational psychologists argued that failure in school is traumatic and students should be passed from grade to grade even if they have not mastered the required knowledge and skills. Many grade and high schools operated on this principle. The few psychologists and teachers who disputed it were classified as unprogressive. Yet now it is being recognized that the struggle to acquire basic reading, writing, and arithmetic skills is much more traumatic at age eighteen or twenty-eight than at age eight.

Avoiding Mindless Conformity

Some people believe that the way to avoid conformity is simply to oppose the majority view. It is not. *Opposing* a particular view because the majority endorses it is no different from *endorsing* the view because the majority endorses it. In both cases our judgment is determined by what others think. And that makes us conformists.

Other people believe that the way to avoid conformity is to ignore what everyone else thinks and decide on the basis of our own ideas alone. This, too, is a mistake. It protects us from other people's foolishness, but it leaves us prey to our own. Consulting informed people, either in person or through their public statements in interviews, articles, and books, is an important part of the process of examining an issue. Other people's views are thus part of the *evidence* we must consider in forming a judgment.

The secret to avoiding mindless conformity is neither to prefer the majority or the minority view nor to be selective in the evidence we consider. The key is to apply our critical thinking to all the evidence and endorse the most reasonable view regardless of who or how many endorse that view.

Applications

1. List some desirable conforming behaviors and some undesirable ones. In each case, explain your classification of the behavior.

2. Describe one or more examples of groupthink that you have observed. Explain what factors were responsible for the people abandoning their individuality.

3. Think of *two* significant ways in which you have conformed with the ways of others. Examine each separately and determine what motivated you to conform. Evaluate the effects of your conformity on yourself and others.

4. Advertising frequently plays on our urge to conform. Describe at least three advertisements or commercials that do so, and explain how they do it.

5. Evaluate the following argument as you did the arguments in Chapter 2, application 7. First identify the argument's component parts (including hidden premises) and ask relevant questions, as shown in that chapter. Then check the accuracy of each premise, stated or hidden, and decide whether the conclusion is the most reasonable one. Note that checking the accuracy of the premises may require obtaining sufficient evidence to permit a judgment. (Be sure that you make your judgment on the evidence and not on the basis of what you feel comfortable saying to your professor or classmates.) If you find a premise to be inaccurate or a conclusion to be less than completely reasonable, revise the argument accordingly.

Background note: Though once allowed everywhere, smoking is now being banned in a growing number of places—on airplanes and buses, in public buildings, in many restaurants. Many smokers feel they are the victims of discrimination.

Argument: Unnecessarily restricting people's right to choose is a violation of their constitutional rights. Restrictions on smoking unnecessarily restrict people's rights. Therefore, restrictions on smoking are a violation of smokers' constitutional rights.

6. In each of the following situations, the person is conforming. Study each situation and determine what effects the conformity will have on that person and on other people. On the basis of those effects, decide whether the conformity is desirable. If your decision depends on the degree of the conformity or the circumstances in which it occurred, explain in what situations you would approve and why.

a. Bert is thirteen. His friends are insensitive to other people and even look for opportunities to ridicule them. If a classmate is overweight or homely or unusually shy or not too intelligent, they will taunt the person about it. If the person shows signs of being bothered by the cruelty, they will see this as a sign of weakness and increase the abuse. Bert knows this behavior is wrong and he derives no pleasure from it, but he goes along with it and even indulges in it from time to time so as not to appear weak to his friends. He realizes that in their eyes, if he is not with them completely, he is against them.

b. Rose works in a dress factory. Shortly after she began work, she realized that the other workers' output was unrealistically low and that she could complete twice as much work as the others without straining. Then, in subtle ways, her co-workers let her know that if she worked at a reasonable pace, the employer would become aware of their deception and demand increased production from them. Knowing she would at the very least be ostracized if she did not conform to their work pace, she decided to do so.

c. Alex is a freshman representative in the state legislature. When an important issue is being debated, he is approached by a powerful lobbyist who informs him that his political career will stand a better chance of surviving if he votes a certain way. The lobbyist mentions the names of half a dozen other representatives and suggests that Alex ask them about the wisdom of voting that way. He contacts them and they say, in effect, "We're supporting the position of that lobbying group; if you value your career, you'll do the same." He takes their advice and conforms.

7. Analyze each of the following issues carefully, and then decide what judgment is most reasonable. Be sure to apply what you learned in this chapter about avoiding mindless conformity.

a. Many people believe that pornography exploits women by portraying them as objects rather than as persons and creating the false impression that they secretly yearn to be raped. Do you agree with this view?

b. Reports of human rights violations (such as imprisonment without formal charges or trial, torture, and even murder) continue to come from a number of countries that receive foreign aid from the United States. Many people believe the United States should demand that those countries end such violations as a condition of receiving foreign aid. Do you agree?

c. When people are stopped on suspicion of drunken driving, they are often asked to submit to a breathalyzer test. If they refuse, their refusal can be used as evidence against them in court. Some lawyers believe such evidence amounts to testifying against oneself and is therefore unconstitutional. What is your view?

d. The Georgia Supreme Court ruled that a church founded by a woman who calls herself "a pagan and a witch" is entitled to a property tax exemption on the building her group uses for worship.[3] Do you endorse that court ruling?

8. *Group discussion exercise:* Discuss the following idea with two or three classmates. Decide how reasonable it is.

Background note: The sport called "ultimate fighting" differs radically from boxing. The combatants use no gloves or headgear, and the contests are virtually without rules. Head-butting is acceptable, as is kicking. If one combatant knocks the other down, he is free to kick and pummel him into unconsciousness. Some states have outlawed ultimate fighting, but it has a growing number of fans.[4]

The idea: Outlawing this sport simply because many people find its brutality distasteful is a violation of the rights of the fans who enjoy it.

9. After your group discussion (application 8), consider what pressure to conform you felt before or during the discussion. Be sure to consider subtle pressure, such as the feeling that your family or friends might disagree with you or the discomfort of having someone in the group dispute your view. Determine what influence, if any, this pressure had on your final decision on the issue.

CHAPTER 9

Face-Saving

Everyone has a self-image, often a favorable one. It's perfectly natural to want to see ourselves affirmatively: as wise, responsible, intelligent, observant, courageous, generous, considerate, and so on. Similarly, there's nothing wrong with wanting to project a good image to others. This desire is part of the larger desire to be good people, people of character, and to live up to the demanding standards that are required.

Unfortunately, those natural and healthy desires often prompt us to resort to face-saving maneuvers. Face-saving is attempting to preserve our self-image or the image we project to others when some unpleasant reality threatens it. The child who loses his temper and punches his playmate, for example, will say, "It's not my fault; she made me do it by laughing at me." The adult who makes a costly mistake at work will explain, "I couldn't help it; the directions I was given were misleading." Both are trying to save face, to find an excuse for their behavior. Similarly, most people are quick to accept praise but slow to accept blame. (A good example of these twin characteristics is the way many students speak of their grades: "*I got* a B" but "*The professor gave* me a D.")

Fully mature, emotionally balanced individuals should be able to draw the line at these relatively modest face-saving maneuvers and not go beyond them. That is, they should be able to resist projecting onto others the share of blame they themselves deserve. Most people undoubtedly do resist most of the time, yet no one behaves maturely in every situation.

Face-Saving Situations

All of us have moments when we strive unreasonably, and often unconsciously, to protect our image. For some of us, those moments occur when a particular aspect of our image is involved. Individuals who pride themselves on being good judges of people may be mature and balanced about many things, but when the candidate they voted for is found guilty of misusing his or her office, they may persist in denying the evidence, scream about the hypocrisy of the opposing party, and predict that in years to come the judgment will be reversed. They may do all of this merely to preserve the image of their perceptiveness in judging people.

Similarly, people who believe they possess unusual self-control may deny that they are slaves to smoking or drinking and strain good sense in defending their habit. ("No one has really *proved* that smoking is harmful; besides, it relieves tension" or "I don't drink because I have to but because I enjoy it; I can stop anytime I want to.") When people who think of themselves as totally self-sufficient are reminded that they owe some-one money, they may find fault with that person for reminding them. Those who see themselves as sensitive to others and completely free of prejudice may denounce anyone who points, however innocently and constructively, to evidence that suggests otherwise. In each of these cases, the people may act to maintain their favorable self-image.

For many individuals the need to save face centers around a particu-lar role in their lives. Sam thinks of himself as a very devoted father who sacrifices for his children and has a close relationship with them. One day during an argument, his son blurts out that for years Sam has been more concerned with his business and his own leisure pursuits than with his children; he has, in fact, ignored and rejected them. Sam turns to his wife and demands that she tell the boy his charge is untrue. His wife slowly and painfully replies that the charge is essentially *true*. Sam storms out of the house, angry and hurt, convinced that he has been grievously wronged.

Jackie sees herself as an unusually bright and conscientious student. Whenever the teacher returns a test paper that Jackie has done poorly on, she challenges the fairness of the questions. If this fails to get her grade changed, she paces the corridors of the school complaining to her friends that the teacher is incompetent or dislikes her because of her clothes or religion or point of view. Those courses from which she absents herself regularly, she tells herself, are boring or useless.

For still others, it is neither the particular aspect of the image nor the role involved that triggers the face-saving reaction. It is the people who are observing. Are they friends or strangers? Parents or peers? Employers or co-workers? What some people think of us we may not care about at all; what others think of us we may care about beyond reasonableness.

Causes and Effects of Face-Saving

Different theories attempt to explain why people feel the need to save face. One plausible theory, proposed by psychologist Alfred Adler, is that to some extent everyone suffers from feelings of inferiority. Building on this theory, Thomas A. Harris suggests that the early childhood experience, with the feeling of being dominated by adults, leaves everyone feeling somewhat insecure and unconfident in later life.[1] This theory helps explain why some people feel such a need to maintain a favorable image that they become defensive about various situations—not only those in which they do look bad but also those in which they might possibly look bad and even those in which their suspicion of their own inferiority makes them *imagine* they might.

As the foregoing examples clearly indicate, the face-saving process can impede growth in self-awareness by locking us into a rigid and wishful view of our personalities. Less obvious but equally unfortunate, it can pose a serious obstacle to clear thinking. By indulging our fears of unpleasant facts, face-saving leaves us indisposed to inquiry. And by limiting us only to the conclusions that reinforce our self-image, it blocks out the full range of conclusions that deserve consideration.

Just how do these effects occur in real situations? Let's consider three actual cases. In the first, I was discussing a thought-provoking article on marijuana with a college instructor friend. The article, which appeared in the *Journal of the American Medical Association*, reported the results of a clinical study of marijuana use.[2] The authors concluded that "contrary to what is frequently reported, we have found the effect of marijuana to be not merely that of a mild intoxicant which causes a slight exaggeration of usual adolescent behavior, but a specific and separate clinical syndrome. ..." The principal effects they noted were "disturbed awareness of the self, apathy, confusion and poor reality testing." They presented the details of thirteen actual cases to demonstrate these effects.

My friend remarked that his own experiences with marijuana while in college showed all these signs and that the changes in his behavior closely paralleled those described in the thirteen cases. That is, he had become somewhat slovenly, irritable, and forgetful; had experienced difficulty concentrating on his studies and paying attention in class; and had suffered frequent headaches. Yet at that time, he explained, he succeeded in convincing himself that nothing had changed in his behavior, that his courses had merely become less interesting and meaningful, that others were annoying him, and so on. Why? Apparently because his self-image—a self-possessed person, very much in control of himself and his behavior, unaffected by his pot smoking—was so important to him that he was willing to *deny his own perceptions and the obvious logic of the situation rather than threaten that image*. So effective were his face-saving maneuvers, he explained, that more than five years passed before he could accept the truth.

The second case concerns a student who was enrolled in a critical thinking class a few years ago. One of the topics for analysis in the course was abortion. A number of exercises were used to identify the various strengths and weaknesses found in the arguments on both sides of the issue (for example, the tendency of many on the "pro" side to ignore the question of at what point, if any, the fetus acquires human rights, and the tendency of many on the "anti" side to minimize the emotional pain often caused by having an unwanted baby). One of the later assignments was to observe a televised debate on abortion between two professors and identify the strengths and weaknesses of their arguments.

This student's written analysis said, in effect, that the "pro" professor's argument had no weaknesses at all while the "anti" professor's was riddled with weaknesses. The student maintained this position in class discussion even though his classmates found significant strengths and weaknesses in both positions. (In fact, a clear majority gave the edge not to the "pro" professor, but to the "anti.") Even after the class listened to a tape of the debate that demonstrated that this student had heard incorrectly in several important instances, he remained convinced that his analysis was correct. The more the evidence mounted against his position, the more strongly he advanced it. "Not giving in" had become a last-ditch device to save face.

The third case involves a college professor. While reading a book that discussed effective teaching, she encountered a chapter that examined a particular classroom practice and showed how it was not only ineffective but actually harmful to learning. As soon as the approach was identified, she recognized it as one of her own favorite approaches. As she read further into the author's criticism of it (she recounted to me later), she began to feel defensive, and even angry. "No," she mumbled to herself, "the author is wrong. The approach is a good one. He just doesn't understand." The professor had nothing rational to base these reactions on— simply the impulse to save face. No one else was around. She was alone with the author's words. Yet defending the approach, and saving herself the embarrassment of admitting she didn't know as much as she thought she did, became more important than knowing the truth.

It's a mark of the professor's character and self-control that as soon as she recognized what she was doing, she checked the tendency and forced herself to consider the author's arguments calmly and reasonably. Surely the temptation not to do so must have been powerful.

Controlling Face-Saving Tendencies

The harm face-saving does to critical thinking is significant. By prompting us to misinterpret our perceptions and substitute wishful thinking for reality, it leads us to rationalize. Rationalizing is the very opposite of reasoning; whereas reasoning works from evidence to conclusion, rationalizing works from conclusion to evidence. That is, rationalizing starts with what we *want* to be so and then selectively compiles "evidence" to prove that it *is* so. Thus, face-saving undermines the very process by which we think critically.

Unfortunately, there is probably nothing we can do to eliminate our face-saving tendency. It is too much a part of being human to be disposed of entirely. Nevertheless, we can learn to control it and thereby greatly reduce its effect on our critical thinking. Here are some tips to help you control your face-saving tendency:

1. Begin by admitting that you have it. In addition, persuade yourself that there is no shame in having it because it is a natural tendency; there is only shame in being dishonest with yourself and denying its existence.
2. Become more aware of your reaction to unpleasant ideas that you hear or read.
3. Try to anticipate occasions of face-saving.
4. Whenever you catch yourself saving face, stop and say, "OK, that's what I want to be so, but what really is so? Where does the truth lie?" By refusing to cooperate with the irrationality within you and demanding that your thinking be uncompromisingly honest rather than merely self-congratulatory, you will soon have your face-saving under control.

Applications

1. Which of the following statements are consistent with the view detailed in the chapter? Explain your choices, and if you reject any, give your reasons for doing so.

   a. Face-saving is unavoidable.
   b. Face-saving is a normal tendency.
   c. Face-saving is dishonest.
   d. Face-saving is harmful.
   e. Face-saving is controllable.

2. We all know that it is difficult to forgive people who have offended us. But the ancient Roman philosopher Seneca argued that the reverse is also true—it is difficult to forgive those whom we have offended. Examine this idea, decide whether it is reasonable, and explore its connection (if any) with the subject of this chapter.

3. Evaluate the following argument as you did the arguments in Chapter 2, application 7. First identify the argument's component parts (including hidden premises) and ask relevant questions, as shown in that chapter. Then check the accuracy of each premise, stated or hidden, and decide whether the conclusion is the most reasonable one. Note that checking the accuracy of the premises may

require obtaining sufficient evidence to permit a judgment. If you find a premise to be inaccurate or a conclusion to be less than completely reasonable, revise the argument accordingly.

Background note: More and more communities are trying to do something about the growing problem of litter, which is not only unsightly but in many cases unsanitary and dangerous. Here is an argument addressing one aspect of the problem.

Argument: Things that have monetary value are less likely to be discarded (or at least more likely to be recovered) than things that don't have such value. For that reason a twenty-five-cent deposit on bottles and cans would virtually eliminate that part of the litter problem.

4. Recall an occasion in which you observed someone resorting to (or at least *seeming* to resort to) face-saving devices. Explain what happened. Decide what triggered the face-saving behavior. Was it the particular aspect of the person's image that was threatened, the specific role involved, or the people who were observing?

5. Recall two situations in which you resorted to face-saving devices. For each, follow the directions for application 4. If you have difficulty recalling any situations, look back at the group discussion exercises in previous chapters. (Chances are good that during one of those conversations someone will have challenged your idea and prompted you to resort to face-saving.)

6. Sherri is a sophomore in college. While she is home for spring vacation, she is very irritable with her parents. She seizes every opportunity to criticize them and their values and manages to take offense at their every comment to her. Just before she returns to college, she causes a row in which she accuses them of never having given her enough attention and love. Her parents are at a loss to understand her behavior. What they do not know is that for the past several months she has been living off-campus with her boyfriend and using the money her parents send her to help support him. Explain how this fact may have influenced her behavior toward her parents.

7. Read the following dialogue carefully. Identify any indications of face-saving and explain what might have prompted it.

> *Teresa:* Abortion is always wrong. There is no such thing as a case in which it is justified.
>
> *Gail:* I just read of a case in which I believe it is justified. I think even you'd agree.
>
> *Teresa:* No way.
>
> *Gail:* It happened in New York. The woman was a twenty-five-year-old ward of the state with the mental capacity of an *infant.* The doctor she was referred to said she was totally incapable of understanding who she was, let alone what it means to be pregnant. The experience of delivery would have been so traumatic and the consequences so tragic, in the doctor's view, that abortion was the only reasonable course of action.[3] Even though I'm against abortion, in a case like this, I'm convinced it's justified.
>
> *Teresa:* The issue in that case is not whether the woman should be allowed to have an abortion but what should be done to the insensitive slob

who took advantage of her retardation and got her pregnant. Capital punishment is too good for creeps like that.

8. A number of communities around the nation have enacted legislation banning the sale or possession of handguns. Many people hail such legislation as an important step toward public safety and the prevention of crime. Many others, however, believe it is a violation of the constitutional guarantee of every citizen's "right to bear arms." Examine this issue critically, taking special care to control your face-saving tendencies. State and support your view of the issue.

9. The U.S. Supreme Court has ruled that state, city, and county governments may not hand over their decision-making power to churches. The Court's decision nullified a Massachusetts law giving churches a veto power over the (liquor) licensing of any bar or restaurant that would be established within five hundred feet of church buildings.[4] Examine this issue critically, taking special care to control your face-saving tendencies. State whether or not you agree with the court's decision and why.

10. *Group discussion exercise:* Discuss the following dialogue with two or three classmates. Decide the merits of Quentin's view. Be sure to check any tendency to face-saving that arises during discussion.

Quentin: There'd be a lot less ignorance in the world today if parents didn't pass on their views to their children.

Lois: How can they avoid doing so?

Quentin: By letting children form their own views. There's no law that says Democrats have to make little Democrats of their children, or that Protestants have to pass on their Protestantism.

Lois: What should they do when their children ask them about politics or religion or democracy?

Quentin: Send them to the encyclopedia, or, if the parents are capable of objective explanation, explain to them the various views that are possible and encourage them to choose their own.

Lois: How can you ask a three-year-old to make a choice about religion or politics or philosophy?

Quentin: In the case of young children, the parents would simply explain as much as the children could understand and say that when they get older they can decide for themselves.

Lois: How would all this benefit children or society?

Quentin: It would make it possible for children to grow up without their parents' prejudices and would help control the number of ignoramuses in the world.

CHAPTER 10

Stereotyping

Stereotypes are a form of generalization. When we generalize, we group or classify people, places, or things according to the traits they have in common. For example, we may say most Masai tribesmen are unusually tall or that Scandinavians are usually fair-skinned. If our observations are careless or too limited, the generalization may be faulty, as when someone says, "Hollywood hasn't produced any quality movies in the past fifteen years."

But stereotypes are more serious than mere faulty generalizations. They are *fixed, unbending* generalizations about people, places, or things. When a stereotype is challenged, the person who holds it is unlikely to modify or discard it, because it is based on a distortion of perception. As Walter Lippmann explains, when we stereotype, "we do not so much see this man and that sunset; rather we notice that the thing is man or sunset, and then see chiefly what our mind is full of on those subjects."[1]

The most common kinds of stereotyping are ethnic and religious. Jews are shrewd, cunning, and clannish, and have a financial genius matched only by their greed. Italians are hot-tempered, coarse, and sensual. The Irish, like the Poles, are big and stupid; in addition, they brawl, and lust after heavy liquor and light conversation. Blacks are primitive and slow-witted. (Often, each of these stereotypes includes a virtue or two—Jews are good family members, Italians artistic, Poles brave, the Irish devout, blacks athletic.)

Beyond these stereotypes are numerous, less common ones, about Swedish women, foreign film directors, southern senators, physical education instructors, fundamentalist clergymen, agnostics, atheists, Democrats, Republicans, Mexicans, scientists, prostitutes, politicians, English teachers, psychiatrists, construction workers, black militants, college dropouts, homosexuals, and society matrons. There are stereotypes of institutions as well: marriage, the church, government, the military, the Founding Fathers, Western culture, the Judeo-Christian tradition. A full list would include even God and mother.

The influence of stereotypes is often so subtle that it escapes our detection. For example, one writer claims that the Reverend Jesse Jackson finds it easier to "complain, picket and boycott rather than talk about [the more important subjects of] black responsibility and self-help."[2] And another writer criticizes the African Americans who continually complain about "slavery in centuries past among people long dead" but are silent about the slavery that continues to exist in African countries such as Ghana, Sudan, and Mauritania.[3] If you were asked to describe the kind of people who would make such remarks, what would you say? Perhaps "white people who have no conception of the difficulties African Americans still encounter in the United States" or even "these writers must be *racist.*" Interestingly, your race is probably not a factor in your answer—many whites, blacks, and others would have the same response. And all of them would be wrong, because in this case both writers are African American!

What would make people, perhaps including you, think the two writers were not only white but also insensitive to the African American experience? The stereotyped notion that all African Americans share the same perspective and opinions or at least that they never criticize one another, especially in public statements; and the parallel notion that the only basis for whites to criticize African Americans is ignorance or racism.

Does every reference to group characteristics constitute a stereotype? No. Recurring patterns of thinking and acting are observable in groups, and references to those patterns are therefore legitimate. In ancient times the Chinese were more creative than most other peoples; in the late nineteenth and much of the twentieth centuries, German industrial technology led the world; in recent decades the Japanese have demonstrated remarkable inventiveness and concern for quality. Furthermore, not all cultural patterns are complimentary. For centuries the Spanish and Portuguese disdained manual labor, thinking it a sign of *dishonor*, and emigrants to Latin America carried that attitude with them. Today Sri Lankans have a similar attitude. The prevalence of this attitude in these societies can be acknowledged without suggesting that all Hispanics and Sri Lankans are lazy. (Incidentally, the pattern of thinking that manual labor is dishonorable reflects illogical reasoning rather than indolence.) As Thomas Sowell points out, the acknowledgment and examination of all cultural patterns, desirable and undesirable, advantageous and disadvantageous, is essential to understanding the success and failure of groups, nations, and entire civilizations.[4]

Facts Don't Matter

It would be nice to think that when the facts are known, stereotypes disappear. However, that is seldom the case. The late Harvard psychologist

Gordon Allport, in *The Nature of Prejudice,* pointed out that "it is possible for a stereotype to grow in defiance of *all* evidence...."[5] People who stereotype don't simply accept the facts that are offered to them. They measure those facts against what they already "know." That is, they measure them against the *stereotype itself.* Instead of seeing that the stereotype is false and therefore dismissing it, they reject the unfamiliar facts as mistaken.

People who think in terms of stereotypes tend to be selective in their perceptions. They reject conditions that challenge their preformed judgment and retain those that reinforce it. Thus, a person can notice the Jewish employer promoting another Jew but ignore a dozen occasions when that employer promotes a gentile. Where the risk of embarrassment or criticism prevents them from ignoring details that challenge their stereotyped thinking, they can, as Bruno Bettleheim and Morris Janowitz point out, employ the exception-to-the-rule argument.[6] "I agree that O'Toole is shy, introverted, and doesn't drink," they might admit, and then add, "He really isn't very Irish in his manner, is he?"

Stereotyped thinking often reveals a technique common to all forms of prejudice: shifting responsibility for judgments from the judger to the judged. "The pattern of prejudiced judgment," as James G. Martin explains, "is to ascribe a certain trait to a group with little or no evidence to support it; to judge the trait to be undesirable; and to hold the object-group responsible for the trait, and therefore blameworthy." When the prejudiced person says, "I dislike them because they are...," Martin concludes, "the person really means, "Because I dislike them, they are..."[7]

Contradictions in Stereotypes

Robert K. Merton has noted that the same set of characteristics can be used to support opposite stereotypes. He observed that, though the identifying terms differ, Abraham Lincoln has been loved for precisely the same attributed qualities for which Jews have been hated: his thrift (their stinginess), his hard-working perseverance (their excessive ambition), his zeal for the rights of others (their pushiness for social causes).[8] And James G. Martin comments on the ease with which a person can invoke the stereotype with the least of details. If we wish to have it so, he observes, "the minority group member who is quiet is 'conceited' or 'unfriendly.' And if he is talkative he is 'aggressive' or 'brash.'"[9]

Stereotypers can move from the most narrow oversimplifications to remarkably fair and sensible judgments and then back again. An example of this phenomenon occurred in a series of interviews Harvard psychiatrist Robert Coles had with a police sergeant. At one point the sergeant made this statement:

"I'm not prejudiced when I say that colored people have a lot of violence in them, like animals. The Irishman will get sloppy drunk and
pass out. The Italian will shout and scream his head off. The Jew will
figure out a way he can make himself a little more money, and get even
with someone that way. But your nigger, he's vicious like a wild leop-
ard or something when he's been drinking or on drugs. They throw lye
at each other, and scalding water, and God knows what."[10]

Despite a generous helping of stereotypes in that passage, at other places
in the transcript the same man is revealed as balanced, thoughtful, and
insightful *even in areas where he is given to stereotyping*. He can say things
like, "I believe you should know the man, not where his grandfather
came from" and "Most Negro people are too busy for demonstrations;
they go to work, like the rest of us."

Causes of Stereotyping

Among the most significant causes of stereotyping is "mine-is-better"
thinking, especially in its extreme form, ethnocentrism. Ethnocentrism—
the belief that one's nationality, race, or religion is superior to other people's—can be present in out-groups as well as in the majority, and in new-
comers to a country as well as in "established" groups. For example, in
the United States the heavy immigration of the past hundred years
brought millions of people who had their own language and culture.
These people understandably tended to remain for a time within their
own groups. Later, when they became assimilated into the general culture, they retained many of their fixed views of outsiders. Traces of ethnocentrism can linger for generations and resurface in movements of ethnic pride. Despite the obvious value of such pride, particularly for groups
whose rights have been denied and whose emotional well-being has been
undermined, it can do great harm.

James G. Martin sees ethnocentrism as "the root of almost all the evil
in intergroup relations." "We are almost constantly obligated to choose
sides in human relations," he argues, "to identify ourselves with one
group or another. There is often no room for neutralism.... One must be
either for or against, enemy or patriot, in-group or out-group."[11]

Another cause of stereotyping is what Gordon Allport calls "the principle of least effort." Most of us learn to be critical and balanced in our
thinking in some areas, he notes, but we remain vulnerable to stereotyped thinking in others. "A doctor," for example, "will not be swept
away by folk generalizations concerning arthritis, snake bite, or the effi-
cacy of aspirin. But he may be content with overgeneralizations concerning politics, social insurance, or Mexicans."[12] The humorist Will Rogers

may have had a deeper insight than he knew when he observed how most people are fools when they venture from their areas of competence.

Effects of Stereotyping

Stereotyping does a great injustice to those who are stereotyped. It denies them their dignity and individuality and treats them as nameless, faceless statistical units of a group. The effects of stereotyping on all who encounter it are similarly disturbing. It triggers their frustrations and anxieties, feeds their fears of conspiracies, and creates a network of suspicion and scapegoating.

Given the popular stereotypes, what is more natural than seeing the Jews as responsible for periods of economic instability, Italians as responsible for organized crime, African Americans as responsible for the decay of the inner city, and radicals and atheists as responsible for the erosion of traditional values and the loss of influence of organized religion. Stereotypes provide a ready supply of simplistic answers to whatever problems happen to be plaguing us at the moment.

Nor do the stereotypers themselves escape the crippling effects of their fixation. Indeed, they are often its most pathetic victims.

Stereotyping cuts them off from reality and cripples their thinking. When they believe that entire groups of people fit into neat categories, they believe a lie that will in time invade and infect their thinking on all related subjects.

Many people see all police officers as corrupt "pigs," all college professors as impractical or misguided theorists, all sex education teachers as leering perverts, and all advocates of nuclear disarmament as subversives. It is difficult, and sometimes impossible, for these people to deal with complex problems and issues when they hold such preconceptions. Consider, for example, a plan that was advanced some years ago to meet the needs of unmarried pregnant women and the poor. Called "shepherding families," it provided homes for the pregnant women to live in until their babies were born (as an alternative to abortion) and guaranteed adoption. It also called for aid to the poor (as an alternative to welfare), in which churches would provide food, clothing, medical care, legal advice, and, in many cases, jobs. Altogether an interesting idea that deserved careful consideration. But anyone who accepted the negative stereotypes associated with the plan's author, Moral Majority founder Reverend Jerry Falwell, would be tempted to reject it automatically.[13]

Similarly, it would be difficult for people to deal fairly with questions of Native Americans' land claims when they see every Indian as a feathered savage, uttering bloodcurdling shrieks while burning settlers' homes and scalping women and children. And how can people be reasonable about the issue of welfare when they see the poor as scheming, lazy, irresponsible, filthy, immoral, wasteful, undeserving scoundrels?

Avoiding Stereotyping

It is not easy to set aside stereotypes that have been in your mind since childhood, particularly if they have been reinforced by ethnocentrism. Yet if you do not set them aside, you will never realize your capacity for critical thinking. Stereotypes will corrupt your observation, listening, and reading and therefore block your understanding.

Here are two tips for freeing yourself from stereotyping:

1. Remind yourself often that people and institutions and processes seldom fit into neat categories and that critical thinking demands that you evaluate each on who or what it is at the particular time and place and circumstance, not on preconceived notions.

2. Whenever you begin observing, listening, or reading, be alert for the feeling that you needn't continue because you *know* what the correct judgment must be. If that feeling occurs, particularly early in the information-gathering process, you can be reasonably sure it is a sign of stereotyping and should be ignored.

Applications

1. Evaluate the following arguments as you did the arguments in Chapter 2, application 7. First identify the argument's component parts (including hidden premises) and ask relevant questions, as shown in that chapter. Then check the accuracy of each premise, stated or hidden, and decide whether the conclusion is the most reasonable one. Note that checking the accuracy of the premises may require obtaining sufficient evidence to permit a judgment. (Be sure that you resist being influenced by stereotypes associated with people who have advanced this or similar arguments in the media.) If you find a premise to be inaccurate or a conclusion to be less than completely reasonable, revise the argument accordingly.

a. *Argument:* Taking animals from the wild and exhibiting them for human pleasure is a violation of their natural rights. Therefore, zoos should be outlawed.

b. *Background note: In 1993 a gay organization took the Ancient Order of Hibernians (AOH), the organizers of New York's St. Patrick's Day Parade, to court. The charge was that the AOH illegally discriminated against the gay organization by excluding it from the parade. The reasoning of the AOH was as follows:*

Argument: This parade honors one of the saints of our church. Our religion teaches that homosexuality is a sin. To require us to include gay organizations in the parade would be a violation of our rights.

2. Review the stereotypes mentioned in the chapter. Select *three* of them. For each, recall an occasion when that stereotype was revealed in the thinking of someone you know. Detail the circumstances in which you observed it. If there were other people present and they reacted to the stereotype in any noticeable way, explain their reactions. If possible, decide what prevented the person who stereotyped from seeing the reality in its complexity.

3. Compose a summary of the chapter for one of the people whose stereotyping you described in application 2. Make the summary as persuasive as you can. That is, focus on the particular occasion of that person's stereotyping and the effects of that error on her or his thinking.

4. List the stereotypes that you are most inclined to accept uncritically (or at least are not quick to challenge). Try to determine what has conditioned you to be vulnerable to those stereotypes. For example, it may have been something you were taught as a child or some traumatic experience you had.

5. Apply your critical thinking to each of the following cases. Be especially careful to avoid stereotyping.

a. A Monroe, Michigan, hospital has a policy that only members of a pregnant woman's immediate family can be present in the delivery room. An unwed couple, wishing to be together at the birth of their baby, challenged that policy in court. The judge upheld the hospital policy.[14] What would your decision have been?

b. Sixty-five percent of all school-age children have working mothers. (Twenty-two percent are "single-parent children.") A great many of these children are latchkey kids, those who come home before their mothers, let themselves in, and amuse themselves, in some cases for several hours. Some of these children must also let themselves out in the morning because their mothers leave for work early. Many latchkey kids are as young as eight.[15] Do you think this is a desirable situation for a child? If not, what would you do to improve the situation or eliminate it altogether?

6. Read each of the following dialogues carefully. Note any instances of positive or negative stereotyping. Decide which view of the issue in each dialogue is more reasonable. (Be sure you don't engage in stereotyping.)

a. *Background note: A born-again Texas businessman and a television evangelist smashed $1 million worth of art objects and threw them into a lake after reading the following verse from Deuteronomy in the Bible: "The graven images of their gods shall ye burn with fire: thou shalt not desire the silver and gold that is on them, nor take it unto thee, lest thou be snared therein: for it is an abomination to the Lord thy God." The objects, which belonged to the businessman, were mostly gold, silver, jade, and ivory figures associated with Eastern religions.*

Cecil: That's a real measure of faith, the willingness to discard earthly treasures out of spiritual conviction.

Ellie: It's more like an act of lunacy. It's a terrible waste of wealth. If he'd wanted to express his religious conviction, he could have done something to help his fellow human beings.

Cecil: By doing what?

Ellie: He could have sold the objects, taken the million dollars, and given it to the needy of the world. Or he could have donated it to a religious organization or a hospital. Instead, he threw it away and helped no one.

Cecil: You don't understand. Selling the objects would have corrupted others. He's a religious man. The Bible told him what to do, and he had no choice but to obey.

b. *Background note: A former Florida policewoman filed a federal discrimination suit, alleging that she was fired because of a sex-change operation. The officer, now a man, charged that the firing violated his constitutional rights and asked for both monetary damages and reinstatement on the police force.*[16]

Christine: If the cause for the firing was as the officer describes it, then it was improper.

Renee: I disagree. A police officer is a public official and should not engage in behavior that disgraces that office.

Christine: What's disgraceful about having a sex-change operation?

Renee: It's sick, strange, and abnormal, and it makes the police department the laughingstock of the community.

Christine: Wrong. The only concern of the police department and of the general public should be the officer's performance of his or her duty. Whether he or she decides to have a sex-change operation is no more their business than if the officer decides to take up stamp collecting as a hobby.

7. *Group discussion exercise:* Discuss one of the dialogues in application 6 with two or three classmates, being alert for any stereotyping that may occur during the discussion. Try to reach consensus on the issues. Be prepared to present the group's view (or the individual views) to the class.

CHAPTER 11

Oversimplification

Simplification is a useful, even necessary, activity. The world is complex. Thousands of subjects and millions of facts and interpretations of facts exist. No one can hope to be an expert in more than one or two subjects. Furthermore, as we have seen in previous chapters, even an expert's knowledge and understanding are limited.

Yet the job of communicating is an everyday necessity. Circumstance forces those who know more about a subject to speak with those who know less. In industry, for example, supervisors must train new workers. In government, experienced employees must explain procedures to novices. In such cases the effectiveness of the training depends on the clarity of the instruction. Complicated matters can be made clear only by simplifying them.

Nowhere is the value of simplification clearer than in formal education. First-grade teachers cannot expect their pupils to grasp the lessons in science and math and English as the teachers learned them. They must phrase the lessons in a simpler way, a way suited to the pupils' level of understanding.

Similarly, if those first-grade teachers take graduate courses, their professors probably don't speak to them in quite the same way that they do with colleagues or in articles for professional journals. The professors simplify. And people who attain such levels of intellectual penetration as Albert Einstein and Stephen Hawking probably must simplify when they talk about their fields to *anyone*.

Oversimplification Distorts

Although there is nothing wrong with simplification, *over*simplification (excessive simplification) is an obstacle to critical thinking. Oversimplification does not merely scale down a complex idea to more manageable proportions. It twists and distorts the idea so that it states not truth, but error. Rather than informing others, oversimplification misleads them.

Let's consider a few examples. The first involves a rather common idea: *"If the students haven't learned, the teacher hasn't taught."* This asserts that learning is the sole responsibility of the teacher. Are there poor teachers? Of course. Do such teachers confuse students and impede learning? Certainly. However, that is only part of the truth, for there are also lazy or uninterested *students* who can successfully resist the best efforts of the finest teacher. When they fail, the blame cannot fairly be assigned to the teacher.

In many cases, perhaps most, failure to learn is too complex to place the blame wholly on either side. The student's lack of effort may be a factor, and so may the quality of instruction. Also significant may be the attitudes of both student and teacher and the responses these attitudes trigger in the other. In any particular situation, there are likely to be so many variables, in fact, that only a careful scrutiny of all relevant details will uncover the truth.

Here is another common idea: *"We know ourselves better than others know us."* Now in a sense this is true. There is a side of our personalities that we keep to ourselves—many of our hopes and dreams and fantasies. Surely no one else can know all the experiences we have had and all our thoughts and feelings about those experiences. Even those closest to us cannot know everything about us.

Yet in another sense others can know us better than we know ourselves. Surely the image we project to others is as much a part of us as our self-image. None of us can really know precisely how we "come through" to others. However objective we are, we remain hopelessly bound up in ourselves, unable to see our outer image apart from our intentions. It often happens that even our own deeper motivations are hidden from us. People who have undergone psychotherapy often learn something about themselves they didn't know before. When that occurs, what precisely has happened? In one way or another, the therapist has probed into those people's thoughts and attitudes (and perhaps largely forgotten experiences), learned something about them, and then shared it with them. In other words, for a time, however brief, the therapist has had insights into the patients that the patients themselves did not have.

Many oversimplifications sound reasonable at first. *"Give people a welfare handout and you make bums of them"* is accepted by many people as a profound truth. Yet it is an oversimplification. People whose problem is not misfortune but laziness will undoubtedly be made lazier by receiving welfare. But what effect will welfare have on a responsible person whose situation was caused by misfortune—say, a man stricken with a serious illness leaving him unable to work, or the mother of two small children deserted by her husband? Surely in such cases welfare can be a temporary helping hand that makes the person no less responsible.

Similarly, the idea that *"compulsory class attendance rules thwart students' maturation"* may seem sound to many college students. Yet it omits an important aspect of reality. Too many rules may hamper one's development, but so may too few. Rules requiring students to attend class do not really take away freedom to cut class. They only make the *exercise* of that freedom more significant. For many students that can be an added motivation to make wise, mature choices.

Causes of Oversimplification

The most obvious causes of oversimplification are simple (unhabitual) error and unwillingness to invest the time necessary to probe the complexity of issues. But there are other, deeper causes as well. One is "mine-is-better" thinking, which can lead us to see issues in a biased way and thus ignore facts that don't support our view.

Another cause is insecurity. If we are intimidated by complexity, we may feel more comfortable with superficial answers to questions. Some people need simple answers, because complex situations and those in which judgment can only be tentative and speculative leave them disoriented.

Still another cause of oversimplification is the habit of seeing only what affects us. When laws were passed requiring restaurants to serve any customer, regardless of race, religion, or national origin, some restaurant owners were angry. They reasoned that people who invest their hard-earned money in a business have the right to serve or not serve whomever they please. That side of the issue was so important to them that they regarded it as the only side. But there was another important side: the right of citizens to have access to public places.

Similarly, when the Federal Aviation Administration published regulations governing hang gliders and ultralight motorized aircraft, the U.S. Hang Gliders Association protested. It argued that the government "has no business regulating an outdoor recreational sport that consists largely of people running and gliding down remote hills and sand dunes." The association was seeing one side of the issue, the side that affected it. Now if that were the only side, this position would be reasonable. But there is another important side to the issue: keeping the airspace safe for all who use it, including commercial and private planes. (The FAA reports that hang gliders have been observed as high as 13,000 feet.)[1] By ignoring that side, the association oversimplified the issue.

A Special Problem: Modern Journalism

So far we have limited our discussion of the causes of oversimplification to the main ones, our own human limitations. Now we'll consider another cause that is growing in significance—the corruption of both print and electronic journalism by entertainment values. Journalists used to emphasize balanced, accurate reporting. Depth of treatment was the ideal, desired even when it could not be fully achieved; speculation, gossip, and unfounded opinion were taboo. But times have changed. Commercial television has shortened the public's attention span. Competition and the desire for ratings have pressured journalists into sensationalism and extremism.

A man who coaches writers for success in the world of talk shows advised one client to give shorter, more dramatic answers: "If I ask you whether the budget deficit is a good thing or a bad thing, you should not say, 'Well, it simulates the economy but it passes on a burden.' You have to say, 'It's a great idea!' Or, 'It's a terrible idea!' It doesn't matter which."[2] Translation: *"Don't give a balanced answer. Give an oversimplified one because it will get you noticed."*

News editors and talk show producers crave the odd, the sensational, the outrageous. (If you seeking an explanation for Dennis Rodman's success in publishing and advertising, look no further.) As Cole Campbell, editor of *The* (Norfolk) *Virginian-Pilot*, put it: "Journalists keep trying to find people who are at 1 and at 9 on a scale of 1 to 10 rather than people at 3 to 7 where most people actually are."[3]

If we didn't depend on journalism for our grasp of current problems and issues, this corruption of the profession would be of little consequence. But we do depend on journalism. It provides the facts and interpretations that underlie our judgments. And when we are given oversimplified and distorted reports, our judgments are necessarily flawed. Prudence demands that we be alert for oversimplification in the media as well as vigilant about our own tendencies to it.

Avoiding Oversimplification

Oversimplification occurs either as a simple assertion independent of any argument or as a premise of an argument. (In contrast, hasty conclusion, as we will see in the next chapter, occurs in the conclusion of an argument.) Avoiding oversimplification simply means refusing to overstate the case for an idea. Before you express any idea to others, first check it for accuracy. If it is not completely accurate, rephrase it. Here is how you might revise the oversimplifications discussed in the chapter. (In each case, of course, other effective revisions are possible.)

Oversimplification	*Balanced Statement*
If the students haven't learned, the teacher hasn't taught. *(The statement is categorical, allowing for no other causes of students' failure to learn.)*	Sometimes, when the students haven't learned, the teacher hasn't taught. *(This statement makes essentially the same assertion, but without ruling out the possibility of other causes.)*
We know ourselves better than others know us. *(Lacking a qualification of frequency or circumstance, this statement clearly implies that self-knowledge is superior in all cases.)*	We know some things about ourselves better than others can know them. *(This is still a forceful statement, but its claim, unlike that of the first statement, is not excessive.)*
Give people a welfare handout and you make bums of them. *(Other, more favorable effects of welfare are ruled out altogether.)*	Welfare can develop a sense of dependency and a loss of confidence in solving one's own problems. *(This statement does not deny that in some cases welfare does not have these effects.)*
Compulsory class attendance rules thwart students' maturation. *(This statement denies the possibility of positive effects.)*	Attendance rules that are too numerous or too rigid can thwart students' maturation. *(This statement speaks of certain kinds of attendance rules, not all such rules.)*

The number of words in an assertion is no index of balance or lack thereof. A short assertion may be quite defensible. Consider these examples: "Astronauts receive intensive training," "Large doses of vitamin D are harmful," and "Haste makes waste." On the other hand, a long assertion may be oversimplified—for example, "African Americans who criticize affirmative action in the private or public sector are dishonoring the memory of Martin Luther King, Jr., and the countless others who have labored to achieve justice for their people." This assertion denies the possibility that criticism of affirmative action policy can be thoughtful or constructive, and that is unreasonable. (Supreme Court Justice Clarence Thomas terms this kind of assertion "the new intolerance" and argues that it is "an attempt to intimidate and silence those who dare to question popular political, social or economic fads.")[4] In checking for oversimplification, consider not the number of words but the scope of the assertion. If the scope is so broad that it rules out known realities or distinct possibilities, the assertion is an oversimplification.

In looking for oversimplification (or, for that matter, any other error in reasoning), you may be tempted to nitpick. When someone says, "A series of tourist slayings in Florida in 1993 hurt the tourist industry there," you could say, "That's an oversimplification. The tourist industry was hurt mainly in the cities where those killings occurred. The rest of the state was less affected." You'd have a point, but it would be so minuscule that it might not be worth making. Nowhere is it written that to be a critical thinker, one must be a pest.

Applications

1. Which of the following do you think the author would cite as causes of oversimplification? Explain why you think so, with references to the text where appropriate.

   a. "mine-is-better" thinking

   b. peer pressure

   c. unwillingness to be tentative

   d. one-sided perspective

   e. uneasiness with complexity

   f. intellectual laziness

2. Evaluate the following argument as you did the arguments in Chapter 2, application 7. First identify the argument's component parts (including hidden premises) and ask relevant questions, as shown in that chapter. Then check the accuracy of each premise, stated or hidden, and decide whether the conclusion is the most reasonable one. Note that checking the accuracy of the premises may require obtaining sufficient evidence to permit a judgment. (Be careful to avoid oversimplification.) If you find a premise to be inaccurate or a conclusion to be less than completely reasonable, revise the argument accordingly.

Background note: From time to time people have challenged the recitation of the Pledge of Allegiance in public schools. Their objection is usually to the words "under God." Their reasoning is as follows:

Argument: A public school recitation that claims the United States is "under God" is an endorsement of religion and thus violates the constitutional requirement that church and state be kept separate. Therefore, the recitation of the Pledge of Allegiance should not be permitted.

3. Analyze the following ideas. Decide whether each is an oversimplification. Explain your reasoning carefully.

   a. "I need only consult with myself with regard to what I wish to do; what I feel to be right is right, what I feel to be wrong is wrong." (Jean-Jacques Rousseau)

   b. Elected officials should be held accountable to a higher ethical standard than the average citizen is.

   c. Guns don't kill people; people kill people.

4. Apply your critical thinking to each of the following cases, being sure to avoid oversimplification.

a. Some people argue that when elderly people are too poor or ill to care for themselves, their grown children should be financially responsible for their care. Do you agree?

b. West Palm Beach, Florida, passed an ordinance designed to combat street prostitution. The ordinance authorizes impounding the cars of anyone charged with soliciting a prostitute. The cars can be reclaimed by paying a $500 fine. Its success prompted at least one other city, Tampa, to consider a similar ordinance. Is this a reasonable approach to the problem?[5]

c. The U.S. Supreme Court has ruled that states must provide free public education not only to all children of citizens and aliens legally residing in this country but to the children of *illegal* aliens as well.[6] Do you support this decision?

d. As many as 50 percent of those teaching high school math and science lack the proper qualifications. The problem is that qualified math and science teachers are leaving teaching for higher-paying jobs in business and industry. To attract qualified teachers, some experts propose that schools offer math and science teachers a special salary scale, higher than that offered to teachers in other disciplines. Do you support this proposal?

e. In some states the law now requires motorists to secure in an approved child restraint seat each young child riding in their cars. Do you support such mandatory restraint laws?

f. Some conservative Christian churches practice snake handling as a part of their religious rituals. That is, they pass poisonous snakes like moccasins and rattlers from one person to another as a test of their religious faith. This practice of snake handling, however, is illegal in the great majority of states. Should it be legalized?

g. Women employees of the National Broadcasting Company are eligible for six months of maternity leave with job and seniority guarantees. However, when a male engineer with the company applied for paternity leave with the same guarantees (so that he could care for his baby and ease his wife's return to work), he was turned down.[7] Is the idea of paternity leave a reasonable one?

h. A minister in Hoffman Estates, Illinois, proposed some years ago that convicted murderers be executed publicly on prime time television. The shock of seeing such executions, he reasoned, would deter others from crime.[8] Do you agree?

i. Laboratories have traditionally used animals such as rats, dogs, and monkeys in experiments to develop safe cosmetics and to find cures for disease. The experiments sometimes cause the animals pain. Some animal rights activists argue that causing animals pain is never justified. Do you agree?

5. *Group discussion exercise:* Select one of the cases you analyzed in application 4 and discuss it with two or three classmates. Try to reach a consensus, but be careful to avoid oversimplification. Be prepared to present your idea(s) to the class.

CHAPTER 12

Hasty Conclusion

We have seen that oversimplification is an error that typically occurs in a simple assertion or in the premise of an argument. It distorts reality by misstatement or omission. Hasty conclusion, on the other hand, is an error that occurs only in the conclusion of an argument. It is a premature judgment—that is, a judgment made without sufficient evidence. Exactly what constitutes sufficient evidence, of course, varies from case to case. In general, we may say that evidence is clearly insufficient when there are two or more possible conclusions and the evidence does not clearly favor any one of them.

Weighing Both Sides

Here is a quite common hasty conclusion: *"The overall effect of technology has been to dehumanize people."* Many people arrive at this conclusion after reading an article or two lamenting the decline of craftsmanship or the rising rate of crime in cities. A wide array of additional evidence can be used to attack technology—from the character of many of the tasks workers are expected to perform to the development of sprawling suburbs, the emphasis on objects rather than human relationships, the increase in personal mobility, and the resulting erosion of family life and traditional family values.

However, even this impressive evidence would not be sufficient to support the conclusion. Any judgment about the "net or overall effect" demands a weighing of both sides, the pluses and the minuses. Specifically, what is needed, then, is the other side of the issue—the *favorable* effects of technological advance. If we were to look for such balancing effects, we'd find that technology has decreased the burden of extreme physical labor for millions of people. It has cut the fourteen- to sixteen-hour workday in half and given people time to invest in other pursuits. It has given us electric lights and central heating and the means to travel long distances quickly and comfortably. It has conquered plague

104

and famine. Any judgment of technology that does not weigh these and other advantages against the shortcomings is inadequate.

Hasty conclusions are not an affliction only of the uneducated. They are also found among the highly educated—even among serious scholars. The reason is that hasty conclusions are a consequence of the human condition. In other words, they are made possible by our own natural tendencies and the difficulty of obtaining evidence.

The Harm Can Be Great

The effects of hasty conclusions can be serious and long-lasting, particularly when they are committed by people of influence. During World War I psychometrists administered intelligence tests to almost two million U.S. army recruits. The scores were expressed in terms of mental age. Approximate group scores were as follows: immigrants from northern Europe, 13; immigrants from southern and central Europe, 11; U.S.-born blacks, 10. Careful thinkers would have asked the following questions (among others) before drawing any conclusions. The answers they would have found are in parentheses.

1. Was the test properly administered? (*No. The directions varied from site to site; some recruits were told to finish each part, while others were not. In some test rooms, recruits in the rear could not hear the instructions.*)
2. Were recruits who couldn't speak English, and those who lacked the basic literacy skills, given special tests? (*The original plan called for different forms of the test. In practice, however, this plan was not carried out. Virtually everyone took the same test.*)
3. Were the scores adjusted to compensate for the flaws in the test? For example, were the scores of those who couldn't speak English and those who were illiterate excluded from the calculations to determine group averages? (*No.*)
4. Other than innate mental deficiency, what could explain the superior performance of white northern Europeans over white central and southern Europeans and blacks? (*On average, northern Europeans had been in this country twenty or more years, and therefore were relatively well educated and fluent in English. In contrast, southern and central Europeans had arrived more recently and were neither as well educated nor fluent in English. And many U.S.-born blacks had been denied the opportunity to become educated.*)

Alas, instead of asking these questions, the psychometrists leaped to the conclusion that southern Europeans and blacks are mentally deficient, even though that conclusion clearly implied that *half or more of the U.S. population were "morons,"* a term that was considered scientific at that time. This hasty conclusion was instrumental in the framing of the immigration law passed in 1924, which discriminated against southern and central Europeans. It also reinforced negative stereotypes of African Americans. Incidentally, many of the psychometrists who embraced this pathetically shallow view went on to popularize the use of the IQ test in education. One of them, Carl Brigham, later developed the College Entrance Board's Scholastic Aptitude Test (SAT). [1]

Causes of Hasty Conclusions

Some people's major concern in thinking is convenience. They are afraid of arduous analysis and rattled by complexity. As a result they leap at the first conclusion that occurs to them. They may hear someone say that gasoline prices are contrived by the oil companies and corrupt government officials, and so they accept that conclusion uncritically. After repeating it a few times, they harden it into an article of faith.

Compounding this tendency is the desire to sound authoritative. Feeling some insecurity and wanting to compensate for it, or wanting to make their conversation livelier, many people habitually escalate every statement to a higher level of generalization. "A teenager was behaving very boisterously in the supermarket yesterday" becomes "Today's teenagers are very boisterous." "Mr. Easel, the art teacher at the local high school, gave my son an unfairly low grade" becomes "Teachers aren't fair in their grading." In a thousand different ways, "one" becomes "many" or "all," and "once" becomes "often" or "always."

Even people who have managed to get beyond convenience thinking to greater intellectual maturity cannot escape another normal tendency— the tendency to prefer, in certain matters, one idea over all others. People may be fully conscious of this tendency, even as it is exerting its pull on their thinking. Or they may be completely unaware of it. In the latter case, of course, they are more likely to be affected by it. But either way its attraction is powerful.

Many celebrity magazine and tabloid readers fall prey to this tendency. They stand ready to embrace any report, however farfetched, of scandalous behavior among celebrities. If the celebrity denies the allegation, their belief may be intensified! Undoubtedly, many of the conclusions they eagerly accept reinforce their own deep desires and fantasies. Almost certainly, their conclusions support their view of life and human nature.

Here's how one's preferences can influence one's judgment. Two businessmen have just concluded an extended conference and are having a late dinner in a crowded restaurant. Across the room they notice an acquaintance dining with a woman. They realize she is not the man's wife. The first businessman has had several extramarital affairs himself and assumes other people behave similarly. He is also erotically stimulated by the idea that the couple are cheating on their mates. He concludes that they are.

The second businessman likes to think well of people. He is also very disturbed by the thought of any kind of dishonesty, including marital infidelity. He concludes that the couple are innocent of any wrongdoing.

Which conclusion is reasonable? Neither. In the absence of additional evidence, both are hasty conclusions. It may be that the couple are having an affair. Or it may not. (Any number of other reasons could explain their being together.) So the only reasonable reaction is not to draw any conclusion at that time.

Getting the Facts

The difficulty of obtaining evidence can prompt even careful thinkers to draw conclusions hastily. Examples occur in every field of thought and work. One good example is a problem that drug manufacturers face. Every new drug must be thoroughly tested and proved safe for people to take before it can be released on the market. But testing is expensive and time-consuming. Furthermore, competition with other firms in the industry encourages speedy research. For these reasons it is tempting to judge a drug prematurely.

In the 1960s the most tragic example of this tendency involved the drug thalidomide, which was branded safe and sold to thousands of pregnant women around the world. Only when hundreds of babies were born deformed, some grotesquely so, was the harmfulness of the drug recognized. In the 1970s the "safe" drug Innovar began to be used as an anesthetic. It was soon discovered that a number of people apparently suffered extensive paralysis and brain damage from it.[2]

How much drug testing is enough? It is a difficult question. A drug called Intal has been effective in controlling the symptoms of asthma. An aerosol, it is sprayed into the bronchial passages. It desensitizes these passages so they no longer constrict when allergens (pollen, for instance) are inhaled. During the early testing of this drug, one group of monkeys developed kidney lesions after being administered the drug. Was the reaction coincidental to the use of the drug, or did the drug cause the lesions? More testing was done, but the kidney lesions did not occur, so the conclusion was drawn that the lesions in the early testing had probably been coincidental.

It is possible that the conclusion about the drug Intal may be proved incorrect in the future. However, that would not mean that the original conclusion had been hasty. Rather, it would mean that new evidence was discovered that did not exist earlier and could not reasonably have been anticipated.

Avoiding Hasty Conclusions

We should avoid hasty conclusions because they are insupportable and because, once we form any conclusion, our curiosity in the matter is diminished. In other words, we make up our mind, and before we can even entertain a different conclusion, we must first *unmake* our mind. "Mine-is-better" thinking, resistance to change, and face-saving make that difficult.

Here are three suggestions that can help you avoid hasty conclusions in your thinking:

1. Before you draw any conclusion, be sure you have identified *and answered* all important questions pertaining to the issue.
2. Where you cannot obtain sufficient evidence, either withhold judgment or (if circumstances require an immediate judgment) use the "If... then" approach. For example, if the issue concerns what punishment would be most appropriate for a murderer and you lack some important details about the case, you might say, "*If* the murderer acted in the heat of anger, without any premeditation, *then* I believe he deserves leniency. However, *if* he visited the victim with the clear intention of harming her, *then* I believe his punishment should be severe."
3. Where the evidence will support probability but not certainty, make your conclusion reflect that fact. That is, admit that it is impossible to say for sure what the right conclusion is, and explain why that is so. Then say what the right conclusion *probably* is.

Applications

1. In late August, the Lees, a Chinese-American family, moved into Louise's neighborhood and Louise became acquainted with one of the children, Susan, a girl her own age. A week later, during school registration, Louise passed Susan in the hall, but Susan didn't even look at her. Which of the following conclusions was Louise justified in drawing? (You may select more than one or reject all of them.) Explain your answer with appropriate references to the chapter.

   a. Susan behaved rudely.

   b. Susan is a rude person.

   c. The Lees are a rude family.

   d. Chinese-Americans are rude.

e. The Chinese are rude.

f. Asians are rude

2. Evaluate the following argument as you did the arguments in Chapter 2, application 7. First identify the argument's component parts (including hidden premises) and ask relevant questions, as shown in that chapter. Then check the accuracy of each premise, stated or hidden, and decide whether the conclusion is the most reasonable one. Note that checking the accuracy of the premises may require obtaining sufficient evidence to permit a judgment. (Be careful to avoid forming a hasty conclusion.) If you find a premise to be inaccurate or a conclusion to be less than completely reasonable, revise the argument accordingly.

Background note: Despite the fact that Cuba's AIDS policy has been much more successful than the U.S. policy, it remains controversial. When Cuban citizens test positive for AIDS, they are taken to a sanitarium, where they are fed and housed very well and given the best AIDS medicine; however, they are not allowed to leave.[3] This policy is based on the following reasoning.

Argument: AIDS is an easily transmitted—and at present, incurable—disease, so the suspension of victims' freedom of movement and association is necessary for the good of the Cuban people as a whole.

3. Examine each of the following conclusions. Decide the specific kind and amount of information that it would be necessary to obtain before the conclusion would be justified. Determine whether another possible conclusion might be more supportable than this one.

a. There are many broken homes today, crimes of violence are increasing at an alarming rate, and pornography is flooding our country because religion has been shut out of the schools.

b. Many people have spoken out in recent years for a reduction in U.S. military spending. This is madness. We need to spend every dollar we are spending to maintain our national security.

c. People are willing to speak out against lawful authority and attack the representatives of that authority—police officers, judges, members of Congress, presidents—for only one reason: lack of respect for authority.

d. European and American cultures traditionally have been strongly opposed to premarital sex for one simple reason: *prudishness.*

4. While reading her evening newspaper, Jean notices that her congressional representative has voted against a highway proposal that would bring revenue to the area. She recalls that a recent poll of the voters in the district revealed that 63 percent favor the proposal. Concluding that the representative has violated the people's trust, Jean composes an angry letter reminding the representative of his obligation to support the will of the majority. Is Jean guilty of drawing a hasty conclusion? Explain your answer.

5. Ramona and Stuart are arguing over whether their ten-year-old son should have certain duties around the home, such as taking out the garbage and mowing the lawn. Ramona thinks he should. Stuart's response is as follows: "When I was a kid, a close friend of mine was so busy with household chores that he could never play with the rest of the guys. He always had a hurt look on

his face then, and as he got older, he became increasingly bitter about it. I vowed a long time ago that I would never burden my son with duties and responsibilities. He'll have more than enough of them when he grows up." Evaluate Stuart's conclusion in light of the chapter.

6. Apply your critical thinking to the following cases. Be especially careful to avoid hasty conclusions.

a. An Oklahoma man was sentenced to ninety-nine years in prison for indecent exposure. The prosecutor was able to ask for and get such a long sentence because the man had eleven prior convictions for burglary. The district attorney explained, "People are just tired of crime—they want the repeat offenders off the streets."[4] Do you support the sentence in this case?

b. A Connecticut teenager who stabbed a neighbor to death argued that he had not been responsible for his actions because at the time he had been possessed by demons. Despite that defense he was found guilty.[5] Do you agree with the verdict in this case?

c. A New York woman was having an argument with her neighbor over their children. In anger she used an anti-Semitic obscenity. Because it is a misdemeanor in New York to harass others with racial or ethnic slurs, the woman was sentenced to thirty-five hours of community service.[6] Do you think such a law makes sense?

d. A high school anatomy class in Agoura, California, dissects human cadavers as well as cats and frogs. The teacher obtains the bodies from a university medical school.[7] Do you approve of this practice?

e. Some people believe the college degree should be abolished as a job requirement. They reason that because it is possible to be qualified for many jobs without formal academic preparation (or, conversely, to be unprepared for many jobs even with a college degree), the only criterion employers should use for hiring and promoting is ability. Do you agree?

7. *Group discussion exercise:* Discuss one of the cases in application 6 with two or three classmates. Try to reach a consensus on the issue, taking special care to avoid hasty conclusions. Be prepared to present your group's view (or the individual views) to the class.

CHAPTER 13

Unwarranted Assumption

As we saw in Chapter 12, a conclusion is a judgment made after thinking. (It may be carefully or hastily formed.) We reach conclusions through reasoning. An assumption, on the other hand, is an idea we have in mind without having thought about it. It is not arrived at by reasoning but is merely *taken for granted*.

Making assumptions is natural. Every day we make hundreds of them. Students walking across campus to class assume that the building is open, that the teacher is still alive and sufficiently motivated to be there, that their watches are accurate in indicating that it is time for class, and that going to class will help them learn the subject (or at least not hinder them from learning it). Without assumptions we would have to ponder every word we utter and every move we make every single moment of every day. Obviously, that would represent an enormous output of energy. The net effect would be to increase our fatigue to an intolerable level and hinder progress.

Fortunately, many of the assumptions we make are warranted. That is, they are justified in the particular circumstances. In the case of the students walking to class, probably every one of the assumptions they make is warranted. The experience of walking to class day after day and finding the building open and the teacher there with a lecture to deliver has made those assumptions reasonable. In fact, even on the first day of class, those assumptions would undoubtedly be warranted if the school were accredited and had published a schedule stating that the class would be held at that time. (In that case, the justification to assume would not be quite so strong as later in the semester, but the assumptions would still be warranted.)

But what if something unexpected happened? If the class were at 8:00 A.M., the custodian may have neglected to unlock the door to the building. Or the teacher may have become ill that morning and stayed home. Would that make the students' assumptions that the building would be open and the teacher there unwarranted? No. In such cases we would say that the students were justified in assuming that those things would happen, but they simply did not happen. What makes an assumption unwarranted is taking *too much* for granted. For example, if the students had heard on the previous evening's news that the teacher had just been seriously injured in an automobile accident, it would be unwarranted for them to assume he or she would be in class the next day.

Assumptions Reflect Outlook

All the assumptions discussed so far have concerned relatively routine matters. Yet the network of assumptions people make goes far beyond the routine. It is intimately bound up with their outlook on a large and diverse number of subjects. People may assume that the elected officials of their city, state, and nation are honest and work for the interests of their constituents. Or they may assume the reverse. They may go to the polls each November confident that their vote matters, or they may stay home on the assumption that it does not. When a world crisis develops that involves the nation (an outbreak of armed conflict is the most dramatic example), people may assume that their country is entirely in the right, or that it is entirely in the wrong, or that some fault lies on each side.

Many people take it for granted that the teachers in their local schools are adequately trained in the subjects they teach, have carefully and fairly worked out their grading systems, and have painstakingly developed meaningful lessons. They may also assume that the school's administrators are aware of what is happening in the various classrooms, have developed precise methods of evaluating faculty performance, and are applying those methods to identify the most and least effective performances. Others, of course, assume the opposite.

Most people hold similar assumptions about other areas of endeavor: about medicine, law, and other professions, about industry, about small and large businesses, about the numerous organizations found in society. And their general assumptions usually govern their particular ones. The person who assumes that all doctors are quacks will be inclined to assume that the particular doctor he or she visits is also a quack.

Which of those assumptions are warranted? Those supported by sufficient experience. What constitutes "sufficient" depends on the situation; the more general and sweeping the assumption, the more experience is needed. Unfortunately, it is very easy to take too much for granted, to assume something even if we have little or no experience to support it or if our experience leads equally well to an entirely different view.

Popular Unwarranted Assumptions

Many viewers of the Dracula movies assume the main character is purely a fiction. They do so casually, with little or no warrant. But the assumption is unwarranted, for the character could easily have been patterned after a real-life villain. In fact, it was. His name was Vlad Tepes, nicknamed "Draculya" and "Vlad the Impaler." Tepes was a fifteenth-century Romanian nobleman who ruled so cruelly that peasants of the time regarded him as a human vampire. Though he never bit people's necks and drank their blood, he once invited the poor and sick people of his domain to a large feast and then set fire to the banquet hall. Another time a Turkish ambassador who was visiting him explained that it was the custom of his people not to remove their hats to anyone, so Tepes had the hats of the ambassador and his party nailed to their heads. Certainly his most horrible deed was to have the heads of *twenty-thousand* of his victims cut off and mounted on stakes for display.[1]

For decades many Americans assumed that China was a medically backward country. The basis of their assumption was little more than the more general assumption that the Chinese were socially backward. Because China was closed to Westerners, no substantial evidence was obtainable to support *any* assumption about Chinese medicine. So no assumption was warranted. (Since the early 1970s, when visitors were permitted in China, reports have suggested not only that their health care is quite advanced but that in general it is better for the average person than what is available in the United States.)[2]

Similarly, the traditional assumption of most Americans about Native American medicine men and women has been that they are charlatans, dispensing superstition that certainly can't help anyone who is really sick. This assumption is not based on any knowledge but merely on a generally derogatory view of Native Americans. Only in the past several decades have people begun to learn the value of their treatments. The National Institute of Mental Health, for example, established a scholarship program to help Navajo Indians study "curing ceremonials" under tribal medicine men and women. One of the supporters of this program, psychiatrist Robert Bergman, knows a medicine man who "apparently cured a psychotic woman after a modern psychiatric hospital had failed to help her."[3]

When the sexual liberation movement was launched in the 1960s, it was rather widely assumed that sexually promiscuous people were more emotionally healthy and stable than their "straight" neighbors—in other words, that the former did not need the crutch of traditional morality but could choose their behavior freely and independently. Actually, though supported by the existence of sexually oriented magazines, books, and films and by the mood of the time that sexual "rules" were narrow and restrictive, there was no evidence linking promiscuity to emotional health. The assumption was probably grounded more in wishful thinking or acceptance of others' wishful thinking than in any experience or evidence. In other words, it was unwarranted. (At least one study suggested that sexual promiscuity is the reverse of what was assumed: not a sign of strength but of deficiency. Dr. I. Emery Breitner claimed the eighty-eight promiscuous people he studied were lonely people looking for companionship and approval and were using sex as the means to find it. He termed them "love addicts.")[4]

Many people assume that white slave owners in the United States assigned their slaves surnames. This belief is reinforced by the fact that today some African Americans adopt African names. However, the truth is that slave owners "actually forbade slaves to have surnames." In cases in which slaves had surnames, it was because they secretly took them in defiance of their masters, in order "to identify and dignify their forbidden family relationships."[5]

Many people who hold a "pro-choice" position on abortion assume that the right to an abortion is expressed in the U.S. Constitution, that the *Roe* v. *Wade* Supreme Court decision is logically unassailable, and that the "pro-life" position is based solely on religious faith. All three assumptions are unwarranted. Justice Byron White, in his *Roe* v. *Wade* dissent, rejected any constitutional basis for the majority decision, terming it an "exercise of raw judicial power." Columnist and author George Will makes these observations about the abortion issue:

> The 1973 decision gave rise to the legal locution that a fetus is "potential life." The biological absurdity of that is today underscored by the development of fetal medicine.... [Furthermore] *Roe* rests on this doubly absurd proposition: No one knows when human life begins but the [Supreme] Court knows when "meaningful" life begins.... The Court declared a third-trimester fetus "viable" because it can lead a "meaningful" life outside the womb. The Court said states could ban third-trimester abortions—but not when a doctor determines that killing a "viable" fetus is "necessary to preserve the life or health of the mother." (Interesting noun, "mother.")[6]

As for the assumption that the pro-life position is based only on religion, that view has been the *legal* view in Germany since 1975. At that time the Constitutional Court of Germany concluded that "the life of each individual human being is self-evidently a central value of the legal order... [and] the constitutional duty to protect this life also includes its preliminary stages before birth." The German high court reaffirmed this position in 1993, holding that the state has "a duty to place itself protectively before unborn human life, shielding this life from unlawful attacks" and calling for prosecution of anyone who pressured pregnant women into having abortions.[7]

One of the most common unwarranted assumptions is that the present European and American concept of childhood has always existed. However, the only reason Europeans and Americans take the concept for granted is that they have been familiar with it since their own earliest years. That, of course, is not sufficient reason. Naturally, the concept is familiar to them. But they did not experience life in 3000 B.C. or in A.D. 1500, so they have no warrant to assume that people in those times shared all their concepts and values. Indeed, even minimal knowledge of history gives ample suggestion that concepts and values do change over time.

Was this concept of childhood shared by our ancestors back to the beginning of humanity? No. On the contrary, it is a relatively recent idea, dating back only a few centuries. Before that, children were not considered different from adults in their nature and needs. Examination of the historical accounts, paintings, and sculptures of earlier centuries reveals that children were regarded as little adults. They were expected to perform adult roles and meet adult standards of behavior. Moreover, they were included in adult society.[8] The concept of adolescence as an extended period of emotional upheaval and self-searching is a twentieth-century idea that the ancestors of contemporary Europeans and Americans, as well as people from very different cultures, would find strange and perhaps amusing.

Very likely much of the tension between young people and their parents could be eliminated by a clearer understanding of how dramatically attitudes toward children have changed. As in so many situations, however, such understanding can be reached only when the prevailing assumption is recognized and dismissed.

Recognizing Unwarranted Assumptions

It is not too difficult to evaluate an assumption and decide whether it is warranted. The real difficulty is in identifying it in the first place. The reason for this is that, unlike the other problems in thinking we have discussed, assumptions are usually *unexpressed*. To recognize the assumptions in your thinking and the thinking of others, develop the habit of reading (and listening) between the lines. In other words, become sensitive to ideas that are not stated but are nevertheless clearly implied. Consider this dialogue:

Cloris: I really don't understand why people make such a fuss about violence in films.

Mavis: They say that violent films harm viewers.

Cloris: That's silly. I've watched them all my life, and I've never done anything violent.

Cloris reasons that if she has watched violent films all her life yet hasn't done anything violent, violence in films can't be harmful. That reasoning reveals two assumptions Cloris may be unaware of. The first is that the only conceivable way for film violence to harm people is by making them violent. Is that assumption warranted? No. There is another way that film violence could conceivably do harm: by making people insensitive to others' pain and complacent about violence in real life. The second assumption is that Cloris's experience is necessarily typical. This assumption is also unwarranted. The possibility exists that Cloris is an exception—in other words, that most people are more affected by vicarious screen experiences than Cloris is.

One final consideration: You may from time to time experience some difficulty deciding whether you are dealing with an oversimplification, a hasty conclusion, or an assumption. The following comparison should help you minimize confusion:

Oversimplification...	*Hasty Conclusion...*	*Assumption...*
Is stated directly.	Is stated directly.	Is unstated but implied.
Occurs as a simple assertion or as the premise of an argument.	Occurs as the conclusion of an argument.	Often is a hidden premise in an argument.
Distorts reality by misstatement or omission.	Fails to account for one or more significant items of evidence.	May be either warranted (supported by the evidence) or unwarranted.

Of course, the conclusion of an argument may be expressed as a simple assertion. How can you be sure that any assertion is not a conclusion (hasty or otherwise) in disguise? Fortunately, the question isn't worth agonizing over. If the context in which you encounter the flawed assertion is not an argument, call it an oversimplification. Reserve the term "hasty conclusion" for situations in which there has been a rush to judgment without proper attention to the evidence. And keep in mind that though precise terminology is laudable, it is not your most important concern. That concern is recognizing errors and being able to explain why they are errors.

Applications

1. Not many years ago prosecutors in some states required that one or more of the following conditions be met before they would file rape charges: (a) the force used by the rapist must have been sufficient to make the victim fear serious injury or death; (b) the victim must have earnestly resisted the assault; and (c) at least one other witness must have corroborated the victim's charge of rape. What unwarranted assumption or assumptions does each of these conditions suggest?

2. In 1903 the Mercedes automobile company reasoned that the total worldwide demand for automobiles would never exceed a million vehicles because the number of people capable of being chauffeurs would never exceed that number.[9] What unwarranted assumption was the company making?

3. Evaluate the following argument as you did the arguments in Chapter 2, application 7. First identify the argument's component parts (including hidden premises) and ask relevant questions, as shown in that chapter. Then check the accuracy of each premise, stated or hidden, and decide whether the conclusion is the most reasonable one. Note that checking the accuracy of the premises may require obtaining sufficient evidence to permit a judgment. (Be careful to avoid making unwarranted assumptions.) If you find a premise to be inaccurate or a conclusion to be less than completely reasonable, revise the argument accordingly.

Background note: During his presidency, Ronald Reagan formally proposed a constitutional amendment permitting prayer in public schools. The wording was as follows: "Nothing in this Constitution shall be construed to prohibit individual or group prayer in public schools or other public institutions. No person shall be required by the United States or by any state to participate in prayer." Though the proposal was not adopted, many people continue to support it. Their reasoning, like Reagan's, is as follows:

Argument: Prayer should be allowed in public schools because its abolition was a violation of citizens' rights.[10]

4. Examine each of the following dialogues. Identify any assumptions made by the speakers. Be precise. If possible, decide whether the assumptions are warranted.

   a. *Olaf:* Did you hear the good news? School may not open on schedule this year.

    Olga: How come?

    Olaf: The teachers may be on strike.

    Olga: Strike? That's ridiculous. They're already making good money.

   b. *Janice:* What movie is playing at the theater tonight?

    Mike: I don't know the title. It's something about lesbians. Do you want to go?

    Janice: No thanks. I'll wait for a quality film.

   c. *Boris:* Boy, talk about unfair graders. Nelson's the worst.

    Bridget: Why? What did he do?

> *Boris:* What did he do? He gave me a D– on the midterm, that's all—
> after I spent twelve straight hours studying for it. I may just make
> an appointment to see the dean about him.

d. *Mrs. Smith:* The Harrisons are having marital problems. I'll bet they'll be
separating soon.

> *Mr. Jones:* How do you know?

> *Mrs. Smith:* I heard it at the supermarket. Helen told Gail and Gail told
> me.

> *Mr. Jones:* I knew it wouldn't work out. Jeb Harrison is such a blah per-
> son. I can't blame Ruth for wanting to leave him.

5. Apply your critical thinking to the following cases. Be sure to identify all
your assumptions and decide whether they are warranted.

a. A Cambridge, Massachusetts, man got tired of looking at his neighbor's
uncut lawn and untrimmed shrubs, which reached above the second-story
window, and took his grievance to court. The neighbor admitted to the
judge that he hadn't cut the lawn in fourteen years, but he argued that he
preferred a natural lawn to a manicured one and untrimmed to trimmed
shrubs. The judge decided he was perfectly within his legal rights in leaving his lawn and shrubs uncut, regardless of what his neighbor felt.[11] Do
you think the judge's decision was fair?

b. Parents who believed their college-age sons and daughters were being
brainwashed by religious cults have kidnapped their children and had
them deprogrammed. Should they be allowed to do this?

c. Some parents keep their children out of school in the belief that they can
educate them better at home. Sould this be permitted?

d. Many motorcyclists object to the laws of some states that require them
and their passengers to wear helmets. They believe they should be free to
decide for themselves whether to wear a helmet. Do you agree?

6. *Group discussion exercise:* Discuss one of the cases in application 5 with
two or three classmates. Try to reach consensus on the issue, taking care to
avoid unwarranted assumptions. Be prepared to present your group's view (or
the individual views) to the class.

CHAPTER 15

The Problems in Combination

We have seen how each of the problems discussed in Chapters 6–14 occurs in isolation. Although it is common to find them that way, it is at least as common to find them occurring in various *combinations*. For example, "mine-is-better" thinking may lead us to resist new ideas that challenge our cherished beliefs. Similarly, the urge to conform may lead us to accept stereotyped images of people and institutions, and these in turn may lead us to make unwarranted assumptions or oversimplify complex situations. The possible combinations that may occur are innumerable, yet they all have one thing in common: Cumulatively, they obstruct critical thinking more than any one of their component problems does singly.

Examining the Problems in Combination

Let's examine several combinations of problems closely and determine the specific ways they affect the thinking of the people involved.

- Claude is an active worker for his political party. Because he feels a strong personal identification with the party and is therefore convinced that its platform and its candidates represent the salvation of the country, he is unusually zealous in his efforts. One day he is having lunch with Nell, a business acquaintance. The discussion predictably turns to politics. Claude delivers a few pronouncements on his candidate and the opposition. His candidate, he asserts, is a brilliant theorist and practitioner. Her opponent, in Claude's view, is a complete fool. Claude volunteers harsh judgments of the opponent's political record and of his family and associates and rattles on about how the country will be ruined if he is elected.

  After listening for a while, Nell challenges Claude. She quietly presents facts that disprove many of Claude's ideas and points up the extravagance of Claude's assertions. Though there is nothing

personal in Nell's challenge, and it is presented in a calm, objective way, Claude becomes angry. He accuses Nell of distorting his words, denies having said certain things that he did say, and stubbornly clings to others despite the facts Nell has presented.

Let's reconstruct what happened in terms of the problems we have been studying. Claude's initial problem was his "mine-is-better" attitude, which blinded him to the possibility that his candidate and platform were not perfect and that the opposition had some merit. In other words, it made him overvalue the things he identified with and undervalue those he did not. Accordingly, when he spoke about the candidates and the platforms, he was inclined to oversimplify. Then, when Nell called his errors to his attention (as someone sooner or later was bound to do), Claude was driven to relieve his embarrassment through face-saving devices. Because the stronger one's commitment, the greater one's reluctance to admit error, Claude undoubtedly learned little from the incident.

- Alma is very conservative in her dress and strongly resists any fashion change. When miniskirts came back into style, she was scandalized. She was fond of remarking, "Today's designers are nothing but perverts intent on destroying the very idea of modesty and promoting moral decay."

Like Claude, Alma was the victim of a combination of problems. Her resistance to change led her to see only the worst possibilities in the new and to exaggerate the importance of the matter. This perspective caused her to form a hasty conclusion about the character and intentions of miniskirt designers and to overgeneralize that conclusion to *all* designers.

- When Sam was thirteen years old, he didn't really want to smoke, but his friends goaded him into doing so. He took to it well, though, feeling more like one of the guys with a cigarette dangling out of the corner of his mouth. As he progressed from an occasional cigarette to a pack-a-day habit, the cost became prohibitive, and he began to steal money from his parents to buy cigarettes. "Hey, it's either that or do without," he said, "and I'm not about to do without."
  Now Sam is forty years old, married with a couple of children, and still smoking. He has developed a wheeze but attributes it to an allergy. Each new surgeon general's report on the dangers of smoking sends him into a tirade. "They haven't been able to *prove* smoking causes any disease," he argues, "so it's up to the individual to decide whether he'll be harmed by it."
  More recently, when tobacco companies were accused of adding nicotine and suppressing unfavorable test results, Sam defended them. "Those executives are wealthy. They have no reason to harm millions of men, women, and children." What incenses him most of

all is the nonsmoking zones at work, in airports, and in other public places. "I don't tell other people what to do and when and where to do it, so no one has any business telling me."

Sam's first error was being victimized by conformity. His rationale for stealing reveals either–or thinking. (There was an alternative to stealing—get a part-time job.) His attribution of the wheeze to an allergy showed face-saving, and his tirades against the surgeon general's reports contained the unwarranted assumption that individual smokers are informed enough to decide whether they'll be harmed. His reasoning about executives assumed that wealthy people are not tempted to do wrong. But there are other temptations than financial gain, such as retaining prestige and being included in the inner circle of management. Finally, Sam oversimplified the issue of smoking in public places, notably by ignoring the problem of second-hand smoke.

Avoiding the Problems in Combination

When combinations of problems occur, the effect is to multiply the obstacles to critical thinking. One error reinforces another, triggers a third, and so on. Moreover, though such chain reactions usually occur in one area— with Claude it was politics, with Alma fashion, with Sam his smoking habit—they often spread and influence our thinking in other areas as well. A person who indulges in unthinking reactions to one aspect of life will very likely become more unthinking, not less. The reason is simple. Given the complexity of many everyday problems and the general temptation to deal with them in the easiest, quickest way possible, pat, ready-made answers have a certain undeniable appeal.

The first and most important step in solving these problems in combination, like the first step in solving them individually, is to recognize that you are prone to them. They are not the "other person's" problems. Nor do they afflict only the uneducated or less intelligent. They can be found in varying degrees in all people.

Another helpful step is to remind yourself from time to time what each problem consists of and how you can most effectively deal with it. To help you do this, here is a brief summary of all the problems discussed in Chapters 6–14.

The Problems	*How to Recognize and Deal with Them*
"Mine is better"	Preferring your own ideas for no other reason than that they are yours. Remind yourself

that all people tend to regard their ideas that way, but critical thinking demands that you examine your ideas as you would other people's.

Resistance to change

Preferring innovative to traditional ideas (or vice versa). Expect your first reaction to new ideas to be favorably (or unfavorably) biased. Set aside that reaction and judge the idea on the basis of your critical appraisal.

Conformity

Thinking the way others do because of the group or your desire to belong (or, conversely, thinking the way others do *not*, simply because they do not). Base your thinking on the evidence and not on how others do or don't think.

Face-saving

Attempting to preserve your self-image or the image you project to others when some unpleasant reality threatens it. Distinguish between what you wish were so and what is so. Be honest with yourself.

Stereotyping

Making fixed, unbending generalizations about people, places, or things. Remind yourself that most things do not fit into neat categories. In addition, resist the feeling that you *know* what the correct judgment is when that feeling arises early in the information-gathering process.

Oversimplification

Simplifying that does not merely scale down complex matters to more manageable proportions but twists and distorts them. Be sure your views are an accurate representation of reality.

Hasty conclusion	Making judgments before sufficient evidence is obtained. Withhold judgment until you have answered all important questions pertaining to the issue. If you must answer without sufficient evidence, use the "If... then" approach. If the evidence will support probability but not certainty, limit your conclusion to one that is merely probable.
Unwarranted assumptions	Having erroneous ideas that influence your reasoning without your being conscious of that influence. Develop the habit of reading (and listening) between the lines for ideas that are unexpressed but nevertheless clearly implied. Decide whether they are warranted.
Logical fallacies	Making specific errors in your reasoning about issues. Monitor your thinking for signs of these errors, especially when you are planning an oral or written presentation of your views.

Applications

1. Evaluate the following arguments as you did the arguments in Chapter 2, application 7. First identify the argument's component parts (including hidden premises) and ask relevant questions, as shown in that chapter. Then check the accuracy of each premise, stated or hidden, and decide whether the conclusion is the most reasonable one. (Be alert for the errors summarized in this chapter.) Note that checking the accuracy of the premises may require obtaining sufficient evidence to permit a judgment. If you find a premise to be inaccurate or a conclusion to be less than completely reasonable, revise the argument accordingly.

a. *Background note: In recent years an increasing number of people have complained about the level of violence and the amount of sexual material on television. Television industry spokespeople have generally dismissed the complaints, reasoning as follows:*

Argument: Contemporary shows depict life more realistically than shows of twenty or thirty years ago. Our position is that such depiction does not cause or aggravate social problems, so until research proves otherwise, we will continue to produce programming that tells the truth about life, honestly and fearlessly.

b. *Background note: In recent years a number of states have considered enacting "hate crime statutes," which assign harsher penalties for crimes in which the motivation was hatred of the victim's race, religion, or sexual orientation. In other words, the penalty for beating and robbing an African American (or Jewish) victim while shouting racial (or anti-Semitic) epithets would be greater than that for the same act perpetrated against a white (or gentile) victim minus the epithets.*

Argument: The law is a good one because greater emotional harm is done to the victim when the crime is motivated by hatred.

2. Analyze each of the following cases as the chapter does with the cases of Claude, Alma, and Sam:

a. A middle-aged couple, Ann and Dan, learn that their twenty-two-year-old daughter, a senior in college, is a lesbian. They are appalled. They were raised to believe that lesbianism is willful moral degeneracy. Struggling to cope with their new awareness, each begins to blame the other—Ann suggests that Dan has always been cold and aloof with the girl, and Dan claims that Ann has smothered her with affection. After many hours of arguing, they decide that there is a more direct cause of her deviance—the college. "You'd think educated people would be alert to the danger of degeneracy with all the girls crammed into dorms," Ann cries. Dan shouts, "Damn it, I'm going to send a letter to the chairman of that college's board of trustees. I want the dean of students fired."

b. Stephen enrolls as a freshman at Progress Technical College. He notices that he has an eight o'clock English class three days a week. Because he's a late riser, this disturbs him. But when he attends the first class, he notices that the instructor's name is Stein. "Wow," he thinks to himself, "what better break could a Jewish kid who likes to sleep in the morning have than a Jewish instructor!" Over the next few weeks, he seizes any excuse to stay after class, talk with Mr. Stein, and win his favor. For his first two compositions, Stephen chooses subjects that will permit him to stress his Jewishness (and thereby impress Mr. Stein). Soon he decides that Mr. Stein "understands" him. He begins to cut class occasionally and hands in about one assignment out of four. When he sees Mr. Stein, Stephen plies him with pathetic tales of misfortune. His midterm grade is D, but he tells himself that Mr. Stein is just trying to scare him and will raise his grade in the end. Thus, he attends class even less frequently and does less work. Eventually, the semester ends, and he receives an F in English. His first reaction is disbelief. He rushes to see Mr. Stein, who says, "I made clear on the first day of class that students could expect to pass only if they attended class and did their homework faithfully. I'm sorry about the grade, but you deserve it." From that moment on, Stephen refuses to speak to Mr. Stein when he passes him on campus. And whenever the conversation in the snack bar or dorm turns to teachers, he loudly denounces Mr. Stein as a phony.

3. Three Southern California professors of medicine devised a hoax as an experiment. They paid a professional actor to lecture three groups of educators. Armed with a fake identity ("Dr. Myron L. Fox of the Albert Einstein Univer-

sity") false but impressive credentials, and a scholarly sounding topic, ("Mathematical Game Theory As Applied to Physical Education"), the actor proceeded to present one meaningless, conflicting statement after another. His words were a combination of double-talk and academic jargon. During the question-and-answer period, he made even less sense. *Yet not one of the fifty-five educators in his audience realized they had been tricked.* Virtually all of them believed they had learned something. Some even praised the impostor in this manner: "Excellent presentation, enjoyed listening. Has warm manner... lively examples... extremely articulate."[1] Explain what combination of the problems in Chapters 6–14 may have accounted for the audience's gullibility.

4. Determine your position on each of the following cases, being sure to avoid all the problems reviewed in this chapter.

a. When Alabama prisons and jails became seriously overcrowded, a U.S. district judge ordered that more than 300 convicts be granted early release. The group included murderers, rapists, and repeat offenders. The judge's argument was that serious overcrowding in prisons and jails is a violation of prisoners' rights against "cruel and unusual punishment."[2] Do you share the judge's view?

b. U.S. law has accorded most charitable and educational groups tax-exempt status as long as they refrain from lobbying activities. However, veterans groups like the American Legion and the Veterans of Foreign Wars traditionally were regarded as exceptions; that is, they were permitted to lobby extensively on such issues as the ratification of the Panama Canal treaties, Alaskan national parks, national security, and Saturday mail delivery (as well as issues more directly involving veterans) without jeopardizing their tax-exempt status. Then in 1982 a federal appeals court eliminated special treatment for veterans groups, arguing that it violated the equal protection guarantees of the Constitution.[3] Do you agree with this court decision?

5. Evaluate each of the following arguments carefully. Determine what the most reasonable position is and what makes it so. Avoid the problems in thinking reviewed in this chapter. (Be careful not to assume that the view expressed here necessarily contains errors. It may be error-free!)

a. For years criminals have sold the rights to their life stories to publishers and movie producers. The more terrible their crimes, the more money publishers and producers have usually been willing to pay. This practice, in effect, rewards criminals for their crimes. This practice should be ended. The profits criminals receive in this manner should be placed in a fund to be distributed among the victims of their crimes.

b. There is a widespread notion in the United States that the censorship of books and other materials that some find objectionable is undemocratic. That notion is false. If a book or magazine or CD or videotape contains ideas that are philosophically alien to the American way of life, it is not only the right but the duty of responsible citizens to remove it from circulation. This duty is especially strong in the case of our children. We would not stand idly by and allow our children or our neighbor's children to drink poison. We would take it from them and dispose of it. Why should we be any less vigilant about what is poison to the mind than what is poison to the body?

c. In 1983 the U.S. Supreme Court ruled that a driver's refusal to take a blood alcohol test could be used as evidence against him or her.[4] I believe the Court erred in making that decision. One reason for refusing to take a blood alcohol test is knowledge of one's drunken condition. But that is not the only possible reason. It's possible for a sober person to refuse the test because he sees it as an invasion of privacy. In such a case, the "evidence" would probably be interpreted by the judge and the jury as a sign of guilt, and an innocent person would be convicted.

d. A woman wrote to "Dear Abby," complaining that her son was taking his fiancée's name when they married. Abby replied that the young man was an adult and free to make his own decision, so the mother should accept the situation gracefully. In my opinion, this was terrible advice. When a man caves in to his fiancée's pressure in this way, the marriage gets off to a bad start. Besides, there's something bizarre and unmanly about a man's giving up his family name. His family has a right to expect that he will maintain the family name. It has always been so and should continue to be.

e. On some campuses, when damage occurs on a dormitory floor and the person responsible is not identified, repair costs are charged to all those who live on the floor. This policy is unjust. Sometimes damage is done by strangers who are visiting the dormitory. And even in cases where the guilty party lives on the floor, it is unfair to charge innocent people, many of whom may not even know when or by whom the damage was done. If college authorities cannot determine who is responsible, no one should be charged.

6. *Group discussion exercise:* Select one of the cases you analyzed in application 5 and discuss it with two or three classmates. Try to reach a consensus on the issue, but be careful to avoid committing the errors reviewed in this chapter. Be prepared to present your idea(s) to the class.

CHAPTER 16

Selecting an Issue

The term *issue*, in the context of critical thinking, means any matter about which people tend to disagree; in other words, it is almost synonymous with the word *controversy*.* The most prominent issues—the ones we see most often in the news—are moral, legal, and political: Is abortion murder? Should teenagers who commit serious crimes be tried as adults? Has soft money corrupted the financing of political campaigns? But controversies exist in other fields as well: Agriculturalists are divided over the effects of pesticides on the environment. Investment analysts disagree over what percentage, if any, of the average person's portfolio should be in technology stocks. Educators are at odds over the merits of tenure. Legal scholars differ on whether judicial activism is a danger to the Republic.

Speaking and writing about issues are so common and so natural that they are often done too casually. (We noted earlier how the belief that everyone is entitled to his or her opinion has emboldened many people to express views for which they have no evidence.) Critical thinkers, however, understand that care in selecting issues for analysis is an important part of the thinking process.

The Basic Rule: Less Is More

This rule may sound strange, particularly if you are in the habit of choosing the broadest possible topics for your compositions. Fear of the blank page leads many students to this behavior. They reason as follows: "If I choose a limited subject, such as the Tampa Bay Buccaneers' chances of getting to the Super Bowl this year, the latest research on high blood pressure, or the Battle of Saratoga during the Revolutionary War, I may run out of things to say before I reach the required number of words. So I'll play it safe and pick a general topic such as sports, disease, or war."

*The expression *controversial issue*, though commonly used, is redundant.

Any feeling of security this approach may generate is purely imaginary. Trying to do justice to a broad topic in a composition of 500 words, or for that matter in several thousand words, is as futile as trying to pour a gallon of water into a pint container. It just won't work, even in the case of a simple informative composition. And it has much less chance of working when you are analyzing issues, which are at least two-sided and often multisided. This means that many, perhaps most, of the people who will judge your analysis of an issue not only know its complexities but also have half a dozen reasons to disagree with you. A superficial, once-over-lightly, treatment is sure to fail.

The only sensible solution to this dilemma is to limit the scope of your analysis. For example, if the issue has five or ten important aspects, examine only one or two. You will then have sufficient space to address complexities, make important distinctions, and deal with subtleties. This is the meaning of "less is more"—aiming for depth rather than breadth.

How to Limit an Issue

The following approach will help you identify the significant aspects of any issue and decide which one(s) you are most interested in and can explore within your time and space limitations:

1. *List as many aspects of the issue as you can.* In the case of an important, highly controversial, matter, your list may include more than a dozen aspects.

2. *Decide exactly which aspects you will address.* Seldom will you be able to do an adequate job of treating all aspects. The one or ones you choose should not only meet your interest but also fit the occasion and purpose of your analysis and the amount of time and space you have available.

3. *Probe the aspects you are concerned with in one or more clear, carefully focused, questions.* Doing this helps keep the subsequent inquiry focused and prevents you from drifting from the issue. Write the questions out; then, if your thoughts move in a certain direction, you can quickly glance at the questions and decide whether that direction is likely to be productive.

Let's apply this approach to some actual issues.

Sample Issue: Pornography

The word *pornography* is from a Greek word meaning "writing about prostitutes." Its modern definition, however, has no direct connection to prostitution. Pornography is any written, visual, or auditory material that is sexually explicit, although power and violence are frequently recurring subthemes. The opponents of pornography are diverse and include political conservatives, religious groups, and feminists. The controversy that has always surrounded pornography has intensified in recent years. Among the reasons are the increase in sex and violence in movies and television and the appearance of pornographic materials on the Internet. The central question in the current debate over pornography is the same as it has been in decades, indeed centuries, past: *Is pornography harmful?*

Aspect	*Questions*
The audience	Are the users of pornography male or female? Adults or children?
Themes	What categories of sex are included in books, magazines, films, and tapes? Premarital? Marital? Heterosexual? Homosexual? Voluntary? Forced? Adult–adult? Adult–child? Bestiality? What does the work say about the kinds of sex it treats? What messages does it convey?
Business arrangements	In pornographic films, are the actors paid? If so, does this constitute prostitution?
The actors	Is genuine acting talent required for pornographic films? Do many actors find a career in such films, or only temporary employment? Do they look back on this employment, years later, with pride or with shame?
Alleged harmful effects	What attitudes does pornography cultivate toward love, marriage, and commitment? Does it, as some claim, eroticize children, celebrate the brutalization of women, and glamorize rape? Does it make men see women as persons or as objects? Does it elevate or degrade those who read/view it?
Role of pornography in sexually transmitted disease	Does pornography play a positive or negative role in the effort to combat sexually transmitted diseases, including HIV/AIDS?
Free speech	Does the guarantee of free speech extend to pornography?

Sample Issue: Boxing

The *Ring Record Book* lists 337 professional boxers who have died from injuries sustained in prizefights since World War II. In the United States alone, 120 boxers have died from such injuries.[1] With the death of a Korean fighter, Duk Doo Kim, following a barrage of punches by Ray "Boom Boom" Mancini, an issue that had received the public's attention many times previously raged once again: *Should boxing be outlawed?* Like most other issues, this one has a number of aspects, notably the following ones:

Aspect	*Questions*
Boxer's right to earn a living	Would the outlawing of boxing be an unfair denial of the boxer's right to earn a living?
Boxing and mental health	Is the expression of violence that takes place in a boxing match an emotionally healthy experience for the fighters themselves? For the spectators?
The popularity of boxing	How valid is the argument that boxing should be allowed to continue because it has historically been, and continues to be, very popular?
The classification of boxing as a sport	Is boxing properly classified as a sport? That is, does the fact that the contestants aim to strike potentially harmful blows disqualify it from that classification?
Overcoming the dangers	Is it possible, perhaps by modifying the rules or the equipment, to eliminate or at least reduce the physical danger to fighters?
Effects of being punched	Exactly what effect does a punch have on the human body, particularly the brain? What is the cumulative effect of the punches received during ten or fifteen rounds of boxing? During a career?

Sample Issue: Juvenile Crime

For much of this century, juvenile criminals have been accorded special treatment in the courts. Because the emphasis was on rehabilitating rather than punishing them, the charges were different ("juvenile delinquency" rather than assault or murder), as were the proceedings and disposition of the cases ("hearings" rather than trials, sealed records rather than publicity, and lectures rather than imprisonment). In recent years, however, the public has become dissatisfied with that system. Many people are demanding that juveniles who have committed criminal acts be treated as criminals, regardless of their age. The broad issue is usually expressed in these terms: *Should juvenile criminals be treated the same as adult criminals?* However, like the other issues we have examined in this chapter, this broad issue has a number of aspects:

Aspect	*Questions*
Causes of juvenile crime	Are juvenile delinquents alone responsible for their criminality? Are parents and others in society (makers of violent films, for example) also responsible? If others are responsible, should the law get tough with them? How?
The age of responsibility	Is it reasonable or fair to hold people responsible for their actions before they are old enough to understand the moral and legal quality of those actions? At what age does a person reach such understanding?
Similarities or differences between juveniles and adults	Is it reasonable to hold a fourteen-year-old (or a sixteen- or eighteen-year-old) as accountable as a twenty-one- or thirty-year-old?
Effects of publicity on juvenile crime	Will publicizing young people's crimes deter juvenile crime? Will it assist in the process of rehabilitation?
Effects of imprisonment on juveniles	What effects will imprisonment have on teenagers? On preteens?
Differences in crimes	Should all juvenile crimes be handled alike? That is, should the criminal's age be considered in certain crimes (vandalism and shoplifting, for example) but not in others (rape and murder, for example)?
Repeat offenders	Should chronic juvenile offenders be treated differently from first-time offenders? If so, in what way?
Prisons	If juvenile offenders are sent to prison (say, for crimes of violence), should they be housed in the same institutions as adult criminals?

Narrowing the Issue Further

If you follow the above approach and find that even the individual aspects are too broad to treat adequately in the time and space at your disposal, look for an aspect that can be divided and focus on one part of it. (Not all aspects lend themselves to such division, but in most cases you will find some that do.) Here are some examples from the issue of pornography discussed above.

Aspect	Questions	Way to Limit Focus
Themes	What categories of sex are included in books, magazines, films, and tapes? Premarital? Marital? Heterosexual? Homosexual? Voluntary? Forced? Adult–adult? Adult–child? Bestiality? What does the work say about the kind of sex it treats? What messages does it convey?	One way to limit your treatment would be to examine only forced adult–adult sex in a single medium, magazines. Or you could limit your treatment further by focusing on a single magazine.
Alleged harmful effects	What attitudes does pornography cultivate toward love, marriage, and commitment? Does it, as some claim, eroticize children, celebrate the brutalization of women, and glamorize rape? Does it make men see women as persons or as objects? Does it elevate or degrade those who read/view it?	You might focus on one of the four questions rather than all four. If you choose the first question regarding attitudes, you might focus on love, marriage, or commitment rather than all three. Similarly, if you choose the second question, you might select one of the three aspects rather than all three.

By limiting the scope of your treatment, you not only ensure a clearer focus and increase the odds of staying within your competency, you also make the task of analysis more manageable. The fewer matters that are competing for your attention, the less the danger of becoming distracted or confused. Even on those rare occasions when you are able to address more than a single subissue, careful identification of all of them will make your inquiry more orderly and purposeful. Finally, limiting your treatment will lessen the chance of your oversimplifying complex matters.

Applications

1. Apply the approach explained in this chapter to *two* of the following issues. Be sure to select issues that interest you, because applications in subsequent chapters will build on this one.
   a. Is the U.S. federal income tax system in need of reform?
   b. Is the teaching of sex education in elementary schools desirable?
   c. Should divorce laws be tightened so that obtaining a divorce is more difficult?
   d. Is it possible for a sane person to commit suicide?
   e. Are students' attention spans shrinking?
   f. Should prostitution be legalized?
   g. Should the lobbying of legislators by special interest groups be outlawed?
   h. Should all advertising be banned from children's TV (for example, from Saturday morning cartoon shows)?
   i. Is devil worship a threat to society?
   j. Is it reasonable to believe that some UFOs are extraterrestrial?
   k. Are male athletes superior to female athletes?
   l. Is *political correctness* a problem on your campus?

2. The following issues were included in the applications for earlier chapters. Apply the approach discussed in this chapter to *one* of them. (Disregard your earlier analysis of the issue.)
   a. Should all students be required to complete at least one composition course?
   b. Should creationism be taught in high school biology classes?
   c. Should polygamy be legalized?
   d. Should the voting age be lowered to sixteen?
   e. Should extremist groups like the Ku Klux Klan be allowed to hold rallies on public property?
   f. Should prisons give greater emphasis to punishment than to rehabilitation?
   g. Is the college degree a meaningful job requirement?
   h. When doctors and clinics prescribe birth control devices or facilitate abortions for minors, should they be required to notify the parents of the minors?

3. Select an issue that is currently in the international, national, or local news. State it in question form, and then apply the approach explained in the chapter.

Notes

CHAPTER 1: WHO ARE YOU?

1. This section is copyright © 2010 by MindPower, Inc. Used with permission.

2. Peggy Rosenthal offers a slightly different explanation of the same phenomenon: "Even when we think we are choosing our words with care and giving them precise meanings, they can mean much more (or less) than we think; and when we use them carelessly, without thinking, they can still carry thoughts. These thoughts we're not aware of, these meanings we don't intend, can then carry us into certain beliefs and behavior—whether or not we notice where we're going." Rosenthal, *Words and Values: Some Leading Words and Where They Lead Us* (New York: Oxford University Press, 1984), viii.

3. One example of *non sequitur* is a child's answer to his teacher's question "Why do you get so dirty during playtime?" He responded, "Because I'm closer to the ground than you are." Another is the conclusion of a medical authority in 1622 about the treatment of a wound: "If the wound is large, *the weapon* [emphasis added] with which the patient has been wounded should be anointed daily; otherwise, every two or three days." The medical quotation is from Christopher Cerf and Victor Navasky, *The Experts Speak: The Definitive Compendium of Authoritative Misinformation* (New York: Villard, 1998), p. 38.

4. See *Buck v. Bell*, 1927.

5. Stephen Jay Gould, *The Mismeasure of Man* (New York: W. W. Norton, 1981), p. 335.

6. Michael D'Antonio, *The State Boys Rebellion* (New York: Simon & Schuster, 2004), pp. 5, 18.

7. James M. Henslin, *Sociology: A Down-to-Earth Approach*, 7th ed. (New York: Pearson, 2005), pp. 87, 302.

8. Henslin, *Sociology*, p. 401.

9. Daniel Goleman, *Vital Lies, Simple Truths* (New York: Simon & Schuster, 1985), p. 209.

10. Henslin, *Sociology*, pp. 5, 56.

11. Quoted in David G. Myers, *Social Psychology*, 4th ed. (New York: McGraw-Hill, 1993), pp. 186–87.

12. Cited in James Fallows, *Breaking the News: How the Media Undermine American Democracy* (New York: Pantheon Books, 1996), pp. 117–18.

13. Cole Campbell, editor of the *Norfolk Virginian-Pilot*, quoted in Fallows, *Breaking the News*, p. 246.

14. Ellen Hume, commentator, on *Reliable Sources*, CNN, June 22, 1999.

15. Larry Sabato, appearing on *60 Minutes*, CBS, July 4, 1999.

16. Diane F. DiClemente and Donald A. Hantula, "John Broadus Watson, I-O Psychologist," Society for Industrial and Organizational Psychology, http://siop.org/tip/backissues/TipApril00/Diclemente.htm.

17. Cited in Richard Nisbett and Lee Ross, *First Impressions. Human Inference: Strategies and Shortcomings of Social Judgment* (Englewood Cliffs, N.J.: Prentice-Hall, 1980), p. 173.

18. See, for example, Elizabeth F. Loftus, *Eyewitness Testimony* (Cambridge, Mass.: Harvard University Press, 1979, 1996).

19. Mortimer J. Adler and Charles Van Doren, *How to Read a Book,* rev. ed. (New York: Simon & Schuster, 1972), p. 4.

20. Harry A. Overstreet, *The Mature Mind* (New York: Norton, 1949, 1959), p. 136.

21. Maxwell Maltz, *Psycho-Cybernetics* (New York: Pocket Books, 1969), pp. 49–53.

22. Martin E. A. Seligman, *Learned Optimism: How to Change Your Mind and Life*, 2d ed. New York: Free Press, 1990, 1998), p. 288.

23. Viktor Frankl, *The Unheard Cry for Meaning* (New York: Simon & Schuster, 1978), pp. 35, 67, 83.

24. Viktor Frankl, *Man's Search for Meaning* (New York: Washington Square Press, 1963), pp. 122–23.

25. Frankl, *Unheard Cry,* pp. 39, 90, 95.

CHAPTER 2: WHAT IS CRITICAL THINKING?

1. Chester I. Barnard, *The Function of the Executive* (Cambridge, Mass.: Harvard University Press, 1938), p. 303.

2. James Harvey Robinson, in Charles P. Curtis Jr. and Ferris Greenslet, eds., *The Practical Cogitator, or the Thinker's Anthology* (Boston: Houghton Mifflin, 1945), p. 6.

3. Leonard Woolf, quoted in Rowland W. Jepson, *Clear Thinking*, 5th ed. (New York: Longman, Green, 1967 [1936]), p. 10.

4. Percey W. Bridgman, *The Intelligent Individual and Society* (New York: Macmillan, 1938), p. 182.

5. For a remarkably clear discussion of this complex subject, see Mortimer J. Adler, *Intellect: Mind over Matter* (New York: Macmillan, 1990).

6. William Barrett, *Death of the Soul from Descartes to the Computer* (Garden City, N.Y.: Doubleday, 1986), pp. 10, 53, 75.

7. John Dewey, *How We Think* (New York: Heath, 1933), p. 4.

8. Dewey, *How We Think*, pp. 88–90.

9. R. W. Gerard, "The Biological Basis of Imagination," *Scientific Monthly,* June 1946, p. 477.

10. Gerard, "Biological Basis," p. 478.

11. Copyright © 2002 by MindPower, Inc. Used with permission.

12. Copyright © 2002 by MindPower, Inc. Used with permission.

CHAPTER 3: WHAT IS TRUTH?

1. Walter Lippmann, *Public Opinion* (New York: Harcourt Brace, 1922), p. 90.

2. Gordon W. Allport and Leo Postman, *The Psychology of Rumor* (New York: Russell & Russell, 1965 [1947]), p. 100.

3. Quoted in Francis L. Wellman, *The Art of Cross-Examination* (New York: Collier Books, 1962), p. 175.

4. Elizabeth Loftus and Katherine Ketcham, *Witness for the Defense* (New York: St. Martin's Press, 1991), p. 137.

5. *Time,* August 14, 1972, p. 52.

6. "Chaplin Film Is Discovered," *Binghamton* (New York) *Press*, September 8, 1982, p. 7A.

7. "Town's Terror Frozen in Time," *New York Times,* November 21, 1982, sec. 4, p. 7.

8. "A Tenth Planet?" *Time,* May 8, 1972, p. 46.

9. Herrman L. Blumgart, "The Medical Framework for Viewing the Problem of Human Experimentation," *Daedalus,* Spring 1969, p. 254.

10. This section copyright © MindPower, Inc., 2008, 2010. Used with permission.

11. Cited in Robert H. Bork, *Slouching Towards Gomorrah* (New York: ReganBooks, 1996), p. 144.

12. "Back to School," *New York Times,* March 11, 1973, sec. 4, p. 4.

13. "The Murky Time," *Time,* January 1, 1973, p. 57ff.

CHAPTER 4: WHAT DOES IT MEAN TO KNOW?

1. Barbara Risman, "Intimate Relationships from a Microstructural Perspective: Men Who Mother," *Gender and Society* 1(1), 1987, pp. 6–32.

2. S. Minerbrook, "The Forgotten Pioneers," *U.S. News & World Report,* August 8, 1994, p. 53.

3. Carol Tavris, *Anger: The Misunderstood Emotion* (New York: Simon & Schuster, 1982), p. 144.

4. Paul F. Boller Jr., *Not So: Popular Myths About America from Columbus to Clinton* (New York: Oxford University Press, 1995), chap. 5.

5. Boller, *Not So,* chap. 2.

6. Judith A. Reisman and Edward W. Eichel, *Kinsey, Sex, and Fraud* (Lafayette, La.: Huntington House, 1990).

7. Thomas Sowell, *Race and Culture: A World View* (New York: Basic Books, 1994), pp. 92–93.

8. Sowell, *Race and Culture,* chap. 7.

9. A. E. Mander, *Logic for the Millions* (New York: Philosophical Library, 1947), pp. 40–41.

10. Rowland W. Jepson, *Clear Thinking,* 5th ed. (New York: Longman, Green, 1967), p. 123.

11. Karl-Erick Fichtelius and Sverre Sjolander, *Smarter Than Man? Intelligence in Whales, Dolphins and Humans,* trans. Thomas Teal (New York: Random House, 1972), p. 147.

12. Karl Menninger, *Whatever Became of Sin?* (New York: Hawthorne Books, 1973).

13. Thomas Fleming, "Who Really Discovered America?" *Reader's Digest,* March 1973, p. 145ff.

14. "Scientists Say Chinese 'Discovered' America," (Oneonta, New York) *Star,* October 31, 1981, p. 2.

15. "Shibboleth Bites Dust," *Intellectual Digest,* July 1973, p. 68.

16. "Empty Nests," *Intellectual Digest,* July 1973, p. 68.

17. "Psychic Senility," *Intellectual Digest,* May 1973, p. 68.

18. *Time,* August 20, 1973, p. 67.

19. *Nova,* PBS-TV, September 21, 1993.

20. Mortimer J. Adler, "A Philosopher's Religious Faith," in *Philosophers Who Believe: The Spiritual Journeys of Eleven Leading Thinkers,* ed. Kelly James Clark (Downers Grove, Ill.: InterVarsity Press, 1993), p. 215.

21. Mark A. Noll, *The Scandal of the Evangelical Mind* (Grand Rapids, Mich.: Eerdmans, 1994), p. 238.

22. Herbert Kupferberg, "Why Scientists Prowl the Sea Floor," *Parade,* July 29, 1973, p. 12ff.

23. "Beer Test," *Parade,* May 13, 1973, p. 4.

24. Bernard Goldberg, *Bias: A CBS Insider Exposes How the Media Distort the News* (Washington, D.C.: Regnery, 2002), p. 20.

25. http://www.cbsnews.com/stories/2006/02/16/60minutes/main1323169.shtml, accessed August 9, 2006.

26. http://www.opinionjournal.com/extra/?id=110008220, accessed July 11, 2006.

CHAPTER 6: THE BASIC PROBLEM: "MINE IS BETTER"

1. Edwin Arthur Burtt, *Right Thinking: A Study of Its Principles and Methods*, 3d ed. (New York: Harper & Brothers, 1946), p. 63.

2. Ambrose Bierce, *Devil's Dictionary* (New York: Dover, 1958), p. 66.

3. Cited in Thomas Gilovich, *How We Know What Isn't So: The Fallibility of Human Reason in Everyday Life* (New York: Free Press, 1991), p. 77.

4. Edmond G. Addeo and Robert E. Burger, *EgoSpeak: Why No One Listens to You* (Radnor, Pa.: Chilton, 1973).

5. Gordon Allport, *The Nature of Prejudice* (Reading, Mass.: Addison-Wesley, 1954), pp. 355–56.

6. G. K. Chesterton, *Charles Dickens* (New York: Press of the Readers Club, 1942), p. 15.

7. "Theologian: U.S. Too Tolerant," (Oneonta, New York) *Star*, May 30, 1981, p. 15.

8. "Jailed Rabbi Seeks Kosher Diet," *Binghamton* (New York) *Press*, May 23, 1982, p. 5A.

9. Reported on *Good Morning, America*, ABC News, November 4, 1982.

10. "Pregnant Teacher Stirs Town," *Binghamton* (New York) *Press*, December 22, 1982, p. 1A.

CHAPTER 7: RESISTANCE TO CHANGE

1. Ellen J. Langer, *Mindfulness* (Reading, Mass.: Addison-Wesley, 1989), pp. 43-44.

2. Reported in George Will, *Suddenly* (New York: Free Press, 1992), p. 405.

3. Robert K. Merton, "The Self-Fulfilling Prophecy," *The Antioch Review*, 1948, pp. 193–210.

4. Thomas A. Harris, I'm OK—You're OK: *A Practical Guide to Transactional Analysis* (New York: Harper & Row, 1969), pp. 22–23.

5. "Anna Freud, Psychoanalyst, Dies at 86," *New York Times*, October 10,1982, p. 46.

6. Rona and Laurence Cherry, "The Horney Heresy," *New York Times Magazine*, August 26, 1973, pp. 12ff.

7. Martin Gardner, *Fads and Fallacies in the Name of Science* (New York: Dover, 1952,1957), pp. 241, 204.

8. This approach was used in the 1982 California primary and reported in "Game Show Prizes Entice CA Voters," *The* (Oneonta, New York) *Star*, June 4, 1982, p. 1.

9. This idea was tested by an education researcher, Eileen Bayer. It proved successful. (Fred M. Hechinger, "Grandpa Goes to Kindergarten," *New York Times*, October 29, 1972, Sec. 4, p. 11.)

10. The Reagan administration discussed this plan and indicated it was not opposed to it. "U.S. Considering National ID Cards," *The* (Oneonta, New York) *Star*, May 21, 1982, p. 1.

11. Karla Valance, "This Time, the Rebel's on the Right," *Christian Science Monitor*, January 27,1983, p. 1B; George Basler, "Student Paper Urges Theft and Graffiti," *Binghamton* (New York) *Press*, January 25,1983, p. 1F.

12. Harry Atkins, "Football, Hockey Are X-Rated," *Binghamton* (New York) *Press*, December 19, 1982, p. 60.

CHAPTER 8: CONFORMITY

1. Solomon Asch, cited in Carole Wade and Carol Tavris, *Psychology*, 2nd ed. (New York: HarperCollins, 1990), p. 669.

2. "Groupthink," *National Catholic Observer*, January 27, 1973, p 24.

3. Witch's Church Tax Free," *The* (Oneonta, New York) *Star*, April 8, 1982, p. 17.

4. John Marks, "Whatever It Takes to Win," *U.S. News & World Report*, February 24, 1997, pp. 46-9.

CHAPTER 9: FACE-SAVING

1. "T.A.: Doing OK," *Time,* August 20,1973, p. 44.

2. Harold Kolansky, M.D., and William T. Moore, M.D., "Toxic Effects of Chronic Marijuana Use," *Journal of the American Medical Association,* October 2,1972, pp. 35–41.

3. "Abortion Sought for Retarded Woman," *Binghamton* (New York) *Press,* September 23, 1982, p. 8B.

4. "Bar License Church Veto Struck Down," *Binghamton* (New York) *Press,* December 14, 1982, p. 4A.

CHAPTER 10: STEREOTYPING

1. Quoted in William E. Vinacke, *The Psychology of Thinking* (New York: McGraw-Hill, 1952), p. 338.

2. Joseph H. Brown, "A Paradox in Message of the Month," Commentary section, *Tampa Tribune,* February 23, 1997, p. 6.

3. Thomas Sowell, "Black History Celebrants Pay No Heed to Modern Slavery," Commentary section, *Tampa Tribune,* February 23, 1997, p. 6.

4. Thomas Sowell, *Race and Culture: A World View* (New York: Basic Books, 1992).

5. Gordon Allport, *The Nature of Prejudice* (Reading, Mass.: Addison-Wesley, 1954), pp. 189–90.

6. Bruno Bettleheim and Morris Janowitz, *Social Change and Prejudice* (London: Collier-Macmillan, 1950), p. 137.

7. James G. Martin, *The Tolerant Personality* (Detroit: Wayne State University Press, 1964), p. 19.

8. Robert K. Merton, "The Self-Fulfilling Prophecy," *The Antioch Review,* 1948, pp. 201–2.

9. Martin, *Tolerant Personality,* p. 19.

10. "A Policeman Complains . . . ," *New York Times Magazine,* June 13,1971, pp. 28ff.

11. Martin, *Tolerant Personality,* p. 19.

12. Allport, *Nature of Prejudice,* p. 173.

13. Michael J. McManus, "Jerry Falwell Moves into Social Action," *The* (Oneonta, New York) *Star,* January 26, 1982, p. 4.

14. "Unwed Father Barred from Delivery Room," *The* (Oneonta, New York) *Star,* May 14, 1982, p. 2.

15. *Donahue,* WIXT-TV, Syracuse, N.Y., November 18,1982.

16. "Ex-Policeman Says Sex Shift Cost His Job," *The* (Schenectady, New York) *Gazette,* August 28, 1982, p. 14

CHAPTER 11: OVERSIMPLIFICATION

1. "FAA's Regulations Ruffle Feathers of Hang Gliders," *Binghamton* (New York) *Press,* September 3, 1982, p. 1A.

2. Cited in James Fallows, *Breaking the News: How the Media Undermine American Democracy* (New York: Pantheon Books, 1996,), pp. 117–18.

3. Quoted in Fallows, *Breaking the News,* p. 246.

4. "The 'New Intolerance,'" excerpt from Justice Clarence Thomas's speech at Mercer University School of Law, *St. Petersburg Times,* May 30, 1993, p. 5D.

5. "A Needed Weapon Against Prostitution," editorial in *Tampa Tribune,* Commentary section, February 23, 1997, p. 2.

6. "States Must Educate Illegal Alien Children," *The* (Oneonta, New York) *Star,* June 16, 1982, p. 1.

7. "Paternity Battle," *New York Times*, December 12, 1982, p. 57.

8. "Minister Proposes Public Executions," *The* (Oneonta, New York) *Star*, June 16,1982, p.1.

CHAPTER 12: HASTY CONCLUSION

1. For a more complete discussion of this subject, see Stephen Jay Gould, *The Mismeasure of Man* (New York: Norton, 1981), Chap. 5.

2. Ruth Ellen Thompson, "Lawsuits Link Human Catastrophes, Drug," *Binghamton* (New York) *Press*, March 13, 1973, p. 9A.

3. *60 Minutes*, CBS TV, October 3,1993.

4. "Long Sentences Sought for Repeat Offenders," *New York Times*, April 25, 1982, p. 63.

5. "Possessed Teen Gets Long Prison Term," *The* (Oneonta, New York) *Star*, December 19, 1981, p. 2.

6. "Woman Convicted of Making Ethnic Slur," *The* (Oneonta, New York) *Star*, May 14, 1982, p. 2.

7. "High School Class Uses Human Cadavers in Lab," *Binghamton* (New York) *Press*, December 15, 1982, p. 2C.

CHAPTER 13: UNWARRANTED ASSUMPTION

1. Seth S. Oldschlager, "There Was a Real Count Dracula and He Was Not a Good Old Boy," *New York Times*, August 27, 1972, Sec. 10, p. 9.

2. "Visitors Say China Delivers Better Health Care Than U.S.," *Binghamton* (New York) *Press*, July 16,1972, p. 5D.

3. "Navajo Psychotherapy," *Time*, June 12, 1972, p. 68.

4. "'Love Addicts," *Parade*, April 1, 1973, p. 9.

5. Thomas Sowell, *Race and Culture: A World View* (New York: Basic Books, 1992), p. 220.

6. George Will, *Suddenly* (New York: Free Press, 1992), pp. 313, 318.

7. Cited in Hadley Arkes, "German Judges and Undue Burdens," *Crisis*, July-August 1994, p. 16.

8. J. H. Plumb, "The Great Change in Children," *Horizon*, Winter 1971, pp. 4–12.

9. Will, *Suddenly*, p. 89. Will cites Norman MacRae as his source.

10. "Reagan Proposes Prayer Amendment," *The* (Oneonta, New York) *Star*, May 18, 1982, p. 2.

11. "Liberation Lawn," *New York Times*, May 23, 1982, Sec. 4, p. 11.

CHAPTER 15: THE PROBLEMS IN COMBINATION

1. "An Exercise in Educational Flimflam," *Parade*, May 12,1974, p. 17.

2. "Court Order Blocks Big Inmate Release," *The* (Oneonta, New York) *Star*, December 22, 1981, p. 12.

3. "Ruling Strikes Down Tax Exempt Status," *The* (Oneonta, New York) *Star*, March 27, 1982, p. 1.

4. "Tough—But Flawed—Alcohol Tests," *Christian Science Monitor*, March 3, 1983, p. 24.

CHAPTER 16: SELECTING AN ISSUE

1. "Tragedy May Haunt Mancini," *Binghamton* (New York) *Press*, November 16, 1982, p. 4D.